Anonymous

Mother Hubbard's Cupboard

Recipes

Anonymous

Mother Hubbard's Cupboard
Recipes

ISBN/EAN: 9783337329112

Printed in Europe, USA, Canada, Australia, Japan

Cover: Foto ©Lupo / pixelio.de

More available books at **www.hansebooks.com**

Mother Hubbard's Cupboard:

RECIPES

COLLECTED BY

The Young Ladies' Society,

First Baptist Church,

ROCHESTER, N. Y.

Fourth Edition. — Twentieth Thousand.

MAILED TO ANY ADDRESS ON RECEIPT OF FIFTY CENTS.

SCRANTOM, WETMORE & CO.
Publishers,
ROCHESTER, N. Y.
1887.

INDEX.

"MOTHER HUBBARD'S CUPBOARD."

SOUPS.

BEEF SOUP.

Boil a soup bone the day before wanting it; skim the grease off next day, and melt the jelly; add spices to taste, a little brandy, a small teacup of butter rubbed in browned flour, a little vermicelli, and a grated carrot.

Boil three eggs hard, mash smooth, put in tureen, and pour soup over them.   WASHINGTON.

MACARONI or VERMICELLI SOUP.

Two small carrots, four onions, two turnips, two cloves, one tablespoon salt; pepper to taste. Herbs—marjoram, parsley and thyme. Any cooked or uncooked meat. Put the soup bones in enough water to cover them; when they boil, skim them and add the vegetables. Simmer three or four hours, then strain through a colander and put back in the sauce-pan to reheat.

Boil one-half pound macaroni until quite tender, and place in the soup tureen, and pour the soup over it—the last thing.

Vermicelli will only need to be soaked a short time—not boiled.   IDA SATTERLEE.

SPLIT PEAS SOUP.

One gallon of water, one quart peas soaked over night, one-quarter pound salt pork, cut in bits; one pound lean beef, cut the same. Boil slowly two hours, or until the water is reduced one-half. Pour in a colander, and press the peas through. Return to the kettle, and add one small head celery, chopped fine, a little parsley and marjoram. Have three or four slices of bread, fried brown in butter, cut up and put in the soup when served.

MRS. M. K. W.

POTATO SOUP.

Boil in one quart of water a small slice salt pork, one or two onions, six or eight good size potatoes, boiled, mashed fine and put with the pork and onions. Boil half an hour, then add milk to make about as thick as peas soup. Pepper and salt.

Just before taking up, add a small piece of butter; strain through a colander.

MRS. M. K. WOODBURY.

TURTLE BEAN SOUP.

One pint black beans, soaked in cold water over night; add one gallon water, one-half pound salt pork, one-half pound beef, one or two onions and a grated carrot. Strain after boiling three or four hours, and add a little wine, one lemon and one hard boiled egg, sliced, into the tureen. Pour the soup over them.

WASHINGTON.

NOODLES.

Three eggs slightly beaten, two tablespoons of water, pinch of salt; add flour to make a stiff dough; roll as thin as wafer, sprinkle over flour, and roll into tight roll; cut into thin slices and let dry for an hour before putting into soup.

TOMATO SOUP.

One can of tomatoes, one quart boiling water; strain, and add one teaspoon soda, one pint milk, a little butter, pepper, and salt; let it scald, not boil; add two rolled crackers.

SPICED SOUP.

Boil a shank bone of beef all day for a soup of four quarts; one can of tomatoes; boil two hours, then strain; add one teaspoon cloves, one-half teaspoon cinnamon, one-half teaspoon allspice. Mace, pepper and salt to taste. Grated peel and juice of one lemon.

One teacup brown flour, moistened with water, pour into soup and boil half an hour.

One-half dozen eggs, boiled hard; chop the whites, leaving the yolks whole; add to soup when serving.

BLACK BEAN SOUP.

Three pounds soup bone, one quart black beans, soaked over night and drained; one onion, chopped fine; juice of one lemon. Pepper, salt and Worcestershire sauce to taste. Boil the soup bone, beans and onions together six hours; strain and add seasoning. Slice lemon and put on top when served. Mrs. Wm. Pitkin.

MILK SOUP.

Four potatoes, two onions, two ounces of butter, one-quarter ounce of salt; pepper to taste; one pint milk, three tablespoons tapioca. Boil slowly all the vegetables with two quarts of water several hours, then strain through the colander, and add the milk and tapioca. Boil slowly and stir constantly fifteen minutes, and it is ready to serve. Ida Satterlee.

FISH.

TO FRY BROOK TROUT, OR ANY OTHER SMALL FISH.

Clean the fish and let them lie a few minutes wrapped singly in a clean dry towel; season with pepper and salt; roll in corn meal, and fry in one-third butter and two-thirds lard; drain on a sieve, and serve hot.

BROILED WHITE FISH.

Wash the fish thoroughly in salt and water; spread it out flat on a wire broiler; sprinkle with salt and set in a dripper in the oven; bake twenty minutes, then brown over hot coals. Pour melted butter over and serve.

A medium sized fish is preferable.   ELLEN.

BAKED FISH.

A fish weighing from four to six pounds is a good size to bake. It should be cooked whole to look well. Make a dressing of bread crumbs, butter, salt and a little salt pork, chopped fine (parsley and onions, if you please); mix this with one egg. Fill the body, sew it up, and lay in large dripper; put across it some strips of salt pork to flavor it. Put a pint of water and a little salt in the pan. Bake it an hour and a half. Baste frequently. After taking up the fish, thicken the gravy and pour over it.

CREAM GRAVY FOR BAKED FISH.

Have ready in sauce-pan one cup cream, diluted with a few spoonfuls hot water; stir in carefully two tablespoons melted butter and a little chopped parsley; heat this in a vessel filled with hot water. Pour in the gravy from the dripping pan of fish. Boil thick.

SAUCE FOR FISH.

Two ounces butter, one-half cup vinegar, one teaspoon ground mustard, one teaspoon salt, a little pepper ; let this boil, then add one cup milk and yolks of two eggs   Let this first boil, stirring all the time.

FISH CHOWDER.

Cut two or three slices of salt pork into dice pieces, fry to a crisp, and turn the whole into your chowder kettle.   Pare half a dozen medium sized potatoes and cut them in two. Peel a small onion and chop it fine.   Put the potatoes into the kettle with part of the onion.   Cut the fish (which should be fresh cod or haddock) into convenient pieces and lay over the potatoes ; sprinkle over it the rest of the onion, season well with salt and pepper, and add just enough water to come to the top of the fish.   Pour over the whole a quart can of tomatoes, cover closely, and allow about as long to cook as it takes to boil potatoes ; then add two quarts of milk, and let it scald up again.   Season with " Sauce Piquant " or tomato catsup, and more salt and pepper if required.

While the chowder is cooking, break some sea-biscuit into a pan, pour water over them, and set them where they will soften and keep hot.   Dip the chowder into the tureen and lay the crackers on the top.

MRS. WM. N. SAGE.

CLAM CHOWDER.

Twenty-five clams, one-half pound salt pork, chopped fine ; six potatoes, sliced thin ; six onions sliced thin.   Put the pork in kettle ; after cooking a short time, add the potatoes, onions and juice of clams.   Cook two and one-half hours, then add the clams.

Fifteen minutes before serving, add two quarts of milk.

MRS. J. M. PITKIN.

CLAM CHOWDER.

Forty-five clams "chopped"; one quart sliced potatoes, one-half pint sliced onions. Cut a few slices salt pork, fry to a crisp, chop fine. Put in kettle a little fat from the pork, a layer potatoes, clams onions, a little pepper and salt; another layer of chopped pork, potatoes, etc., until all are in. Pour over all the juice of the clams. Cook three hours, being careful not to burn.

Add a teacup of milk just before serving.

MRS. HORACE CANDEE.

CODFISH BALLS.

Put the fish in cold water, set on the back of the stove; when water gets hot, pour off and put on cold again until the fish is fresh enough; then pick it up. Boil potatoes and mash them; mix fish and potatoes together while potatoes are hot, taking two-thirds potatoes and one-third fish. Put in plenty of butter; make into balls, and fry in plenty of lard. Have the lard hot before putting in balls.   A. M.

CREAM OYSTERS.

Fifty shell oysters, one quart sweet cream; butter, pepper and salt to suit taste. Put the cream and oysters in separate kettles to heat, the oysters in their own liquid, and let them come to a boil; when sufficiently cooked, skim; then take them out of the liquid and put in some dish to keep warm. Put the cream and liquid together. Season to taste, and thicken with powdered cracker. When sufficiently thick, stir in the oysters.   I. TEAL.

SCOLLOPED OYSTERS.

Put a layer of rolled crackers in bottom of pudding dish, layer of oysters, drained; season with butter, pepper and salt; so on until the dish is full, then pour over coffeecup of milk. Bake three quarters of an hour.

OYSTER PIE.

One quart oysters, drained; pepper, salt and butter to taste. One quart flour, two tablespoons lard, one teaspoon salt; mix with water for pie-crust. Line the pie plate with the crust; fill with the oysters, seasoned; put over a crust, and bake. BELLE.

SCOLLOPED CLAMS.

Put stale bread in oven to dry; roll fine, then put in dish a layer of crumbs, layer of clams, cut in small pieces; season with butter and pepper; so on until dish is full. Pour over the clam juice; bake one-half hour. Cracker crumbs may be used in the place of bread.

PICKLED OYSTERS.

One quart oysters, drain off the liquid; add one cup of vinegar, one cup of water; let it boil, and skim off the top while boiling. One teaspoon of white pepper, one-half teaspoon of allspice, one teaspoon of salt, little stick cinnamon. Let the spices boil with the liquid; when cool pour this over the oysters.

MRS. C. F. PAINE.

PICKLED OYSTERS.

Two gallons of large oysters, drain and rinse them; put one pint of the oyster juice and one quart of vinegar over the fire, scald and skim until clear; add one tablespoonful of whole pepper, one tablespoonful of cloves, one teaspoonful of mace and one even tablespoonful of salt; scald a minute, then throw in the oysters, and let them just come to a boil.

The oysters should be pickled the day before they are wanted, as they grow tough after standing a few days in the vinegar.

MRS. W. N. S.

FRIED OYSTERS.

Take large sized oysters, drain and dry; dip in egg and bread or cracker crumbs. Fry in hot butter or lard.

SUNDRIES.

HAM COOKED IN CIDER.

Put a pint of cider and a cup of brown sugar into enough water to cover the ham; boil three hours, or until the skin will peel off easily. Remove the skin, cover the ham with a crust of sugar, and bake in a slow oven three hours.

Dissolve a cup of sugar in a pint of cider and baste the ham frequently while baking. If the cider is very sweet, use less sugar.

MRS. W. N. SAGE.

STEWED BEEF.

Have a steak weighing two pounds, and an inch and a half thick. Put two ounces of butter in a stew pan; when melted, put in the steak with one-quarter pound of lean bacon, cut in small pieces. Place the stew pan over the fire; turn the steak occasionally until a little brown, then lay it off into a dish. Add one tablespoon of flour to the butter in the pan, and continue stirring until brown; then again lay in the steak. Add one pint of water, one glass sherry, a little pepper and salt; let simmer slowly one hour. Skim off all the fat, and add twenty button onions; simmer until onions are very tender; remove the steak to hot platter, and pour the onions, sauce, etc., over.

MRS. K. WOODBURY.

MOCK TERRAPINS (Supper Dish).

Half a calf's liver; season and fry brown; hash it, not very fine; dust thickly with flour, a teaspoon of mixed mustard, as much cayenne pepper as will lie on half a dime; two hard boiled eggs, chopped fine; a piece of butter, size of an egg; a teacup of water. Let all boil a minute or two, then serve.

Cold veal is also nice dressed in this way.

BEEF STEAK BALLS.

One and one-half pounds round steak, chopped fine; two eggs, one tablespoon flour, two tablespoons milk; salt and pepper to taste. Drop in spider and fry until done.

VEAL LOAF.

Three pounds of the nice part of a leg of veal, chopped fine; six crackers rolled fine; two eggs, well beaten; a piece of butter, size of an egg; one tablespoon of salt; one teaspoon of pepper, one-quarter of a nutmeg. Work all well together; then make into a loaf, and put into a dripping pan; cover with cracker crumbs and bits of butter. Have a little water in the pan, and baste often until done.

Miss ELLA I. GOULD.

VEAL OMELETTE.

Two pounds veal, and one-quarter pound salt pork, chopped fine; one teaspoon salt, one teaspoon pepper, two crackers, rolled fine; two eggs, eight tablespoons cream. Mix crackers and meat; add the eggs and other ingredients. Bake two hours, covered with a pan.

If you have not cream use six tablespoons of melted butter.

Miss JENNIE MORGAN.

BAKED OMELETTE.

Four or six eggs; beat whites separate; small teacup milk, piece butter, size of a walnut; one tablespoon flour, a little salt. Beat yolks; add butter, milk, flour and salt, lastly the beaten whites. Butter a dish just the right size to hold it and bake in quick oven.

JENNIE MORGAN.

OMELETTE.

Soak a teacup of bread crumbs in a cup of sweet milk over night; three eggs, beat yolks and whites separately; mix the yolks with the bread and milk; stir in the whites, add a teaspoon of salt, and fry brown. This is sufficient for six persons.

MRS. AMBROSE LANE.

SWEETBREADS.

Scald in salted water; remove the stringy parts; put in cold water five or ten minutes; drain in towel; dip in egg and bread or cracker crumbs, and fry in butter or boil them plain.

FROGS' LEGS.

Fry in hot butter or lard.

SOFT SHELL CRABS.

Fry in butter or lard.

BONED CHICKEN.

Boil a chicken in as little water as possible until the meat will fall from the bones; remove all of the skin, chop together the light and dark parts; season with pepper and salt. Boil down the liquid in which the chicken was boiled, then pour it on the meat; place in a tin, wrap tightly in a cloth, press with a heavy weight for several hours. When served cut in thin slices.

IDA SATTERLEE.

CHICKEN PIE.

Two chickens, jointed small; cook them tender; season with butter, salt and pepper; thicken the gravy with flour. Make a crust as for soda biscuit; line the sides of pie dish with crust, half an inch thick; fill the dish with the chicken and gravy; cover with crust; bake half hour.

CHICKEN POT PIE.

Two large chickens, jointed and boiled in two quarts of water; add a few slices of salt pork; season. When nearly cooked, add a crust made of one quart flour, four teaspoons baking powder, one saltspoon salt; stir in a stiff batter with water; drop into the kettle while boiling; cover close and cook twenty-five minutes. ELLEN.

SMOTHERED CHICKEN.

Open the chicken as for boiling; put into dripping-pan, with a little water; season with butter, pepper and salt; cover with another pan and cook until done; take off cover and brown them. Make a gravy in dripping-pan of milk and browned flour; pour over chicken.

CHICKEN CROQUETTES.

The breast of two boiled chickens, chopped; one cup of soft bread, two eggs, two spoons chopped parsley. Mix well together; pepper and salt to taste. Roll six crackers; mix with one egg, well beaten. Make the croquettes into pear shapes with your hands, put in wire basket, and boil in lard.

STEWED MUSHROOMS.

Let them lie in salt and water an hour; cover with water and stew until tender; season with butter, salt and pepper: cream, if you wish.

LOBSTER CROQUETTES.

One can of lobsters, chopped; one cup bread softened with water; two eggs; pepper and salt to taste. Mix all together. Roll fine eight medium sized crackers; one egg, beaten and mixed with the crumbs. Make the lobster into round or pear-shaped balls, and roll in the cracker crumbs. Fry in a spider with lard.

POTATO SALAD.

Chop two quarts of cold boiled potatoes; mix one teaspoon salt, one-half teaspoon pepper, two tablespoons parsley, two tablespoons grated onion, one gill vinegar, one-half gill oil or melted butter; pour over potatoes; stand half an hour before serving.

STEWED CRANBERRIES.

Look them over carefully; wash and put them over the fire, more than cover with water; cover the sauce pan, and stew until the skins are tender, adding more water if neces-sary; add one pound of sugar to a pound of berries. Let them simmer ten or twelve minutes; then set away in a bowl or wide-mouthed crock.

WELSH RAREBIT.

Toast the bread; butter it, and spread with mustard; then melt the cheese and spread over, and put together the same as sandwiches.

RICE CROQUETTES.

One cup boiled rice, one egg, well beaten; thicken with bread and cracker crumbs; then roll in cracker crumbs, and fry in lard.

YORKSHIRE PUDDING.

Six large spoons flour, three eggs, saltspoon salt, milk enough to make like soft custard; pour into shallow pan, in which there is a little beef dripping.

STUFFING FOR TURKEY OR ROAST MEATS.

Mix stale bread crumbs or pounded cracker with butter, salt, pepper and an egg; add summer savory or sage. If wished, oysters chopped may be added. Mix thoroughly together, adding a little warm water for wetting, if necessary.

OYSTER DRESSING.

Two tablespoons flour, two tablespoons butter; brown the butter and flour in dripper; add water to make thin for gravy; boil: add one pint oysters, chopped; pepper and salt to taste.

CAPER SAUCE.

Two tablespoons of butter, one tablespoon of flour; mix well; pour on boiling water until it thickens; add one hard boiled egg, chopped fine, and two tablespoons of capers.

MRS. A. W. MUDGE.

MINT SAUCE.

Mix one tablespoon of white sugar to half a teacup of good vinegar; add mint, chopped fine; one-half teaspoon of salt. Serve with roast lamb or mutton.

MRS. A. W. MUDGE.

GRAVY FOR ROAST MEATS.

After taking out the meat, pour off the fat; add water, season, and thicken with flour.

DRAWN BUTTER OR EGG SAUCE.

Half a cup butter, two tablespoons flour; rubbed thoroughly together, then stir into pint boiling water; little salt; parsley, if wished.

For egg sauce, add one or two eggs, boiled hard and chopped.

GRAVY FOR TURKEY.

Boil the giblets very tender; chop fine; then take liquor in which they are boiled, thicken with flour; season with salt, pepper and a little butter; add the giblets and drippings in which the turkey was roasted.

" ROLLED SANDWICHES."

When the bread is ready to make into loaves, put one into a long bar tin; let stand until light, then steam one hour. Make a dressing of ham, veal and smoked tongue, chopped very fine and mixed with salad dressing. When the bread is quite cold, cut into thin slices, spread with the chopped meats and roll.

RAGOUT OF BEEF.

For six pounds of the round, take one-half dozen ripe tomatoes, or canned tomatoes, and three onions, a few cloves, stick cinnamon, whole black pepper, and salt; cut gashes in meat and fill with small pieces of salt pork; put meat in dish or pan with other ingredients; over this pour one cup water, one-half cup vinegar; cover tightly and bake slowly four or five hours; when done, strain with gravy and thicken with flour.

LAMB COOKED WITH PEAS.

The breast of lamb and salt pork cut in medium pieces, put in stew pan with water enough to cover; stew until tender; skim and add green peas; when done, season with butter rolled in flour and pepper.

PRESSED CHICKEN.

Boil two chickens until dropping to pieces; pick meat off bones, taking out all skin; season with salt and pepper; put in deep tin or mould; take one-fourth box of gelatine, dissolved in a little warm water, add to liquid left in kettle, and boil until it begins to thicken, then pour over the chicken and set away to cool; cut in slices for table.

Mrs. E. H. S.

HAM FOR SUPPER.

Chop boiled ham fine; season with mustard, pepper, beaten yolk of an egg, and oil if desired.

VEGETABLES.

GENERAL DIRECTIONS.

First. Have them fresh as possible. Summer vegetables should be cooked on the same day that they are gathered.

Second. Look them over and wash well, cutting out all decayed or unripe parts.

Third. Lay them when peeled in cold water for some time before using.

Fourth. Always let the water boil before putting them in and continue to boil until done.

TURNIPS — Should be peeled, and boil from forty minutes to an hour.

BEETS — Boil from one to two hours; then put in cold water, and slip the skin off.

SPINACH — Boil twenty minutes.

PARSNIPS — Boil from twenty to thirty minutes.

ONIONS — Best boiled in two or three waters ; adding milk the last time.

STRING BEANS — Should be boiled one hour.

SHELL BEANS — Require half an hour to an hour.

GREEN CORN — Boil twenty or thirty minutes.

GREEN PEAS — Should be boiled in as little water as possible ; boil twenty minutes.

ASPARAGUS — Same as peas ; serve on toast with cream gravy.

WINTER SQUASH — Cut in pieces and boil twenty to forty minutes, in small quantity of water ; when done press the water out, mash smooth, and season with butter, pepper and salt.

CABBAGE — Should be boiled from one-half hour to one hour in plenty of water ; salt while boiling.

POTATOES BOILED IN LARD.

Pare and slice thick eight or ten large potatoes. Half fill a good sized kettle with lard or drippings. When boiling put in the potatoes ; cook until tender and brown ; then take out with a skimmer into a colander to drain off any grease. Sprinkle salt over them. Be sure and not fill the kettle too full with potatoes, as it is better to cook at a time only what the lard covers.

STIRRED FRIED POTATOES.

Put a tablespoon of lard into a kettle ; pare and slice fine as many potatoes as needed. When the lard is hot put in the potatoes and cover closely ; watch and stir frequently, to prevent burning. When nearly cooked remove the cover and brown them ; then stir in salt, pepper and a heaping teaspoon of butter.

BAKED POTATOES.

Pare eight or ten potatoes, or as many as needed; bake in a quick oven half an hour.

SARATOGA POTATOES.

Pare and slice the potatoes very thin with potato slicer; let them stand in alum water for half an hour; wipe dry and fry in very hot lard a light brown; salt while hot.

Mrs. L. Sunderlin.

SARATOGA POTATOES.

Take white Peachblow potatoes; peel and slice very thin with potato slicer; let them stand in cold salt and water for half an hour; dry them, and fry in boiling hot lard, taking out as soon as they rattle against the spoon; salt hot.

Mrs. A. S. Mann.

SCOLLOPED POTATOES.

Use boiled potatoes; slice them thin; put in a pudding dish a layer of potatoes, a thin layer of rolled crackers; sprinkle in pepper and salt and three or four small pieces of butter; then add another layer of potatoes, crackers, etc., until the dish is filled. Over all pour a cup of cream or rich milk. Bake from one-half to three-quarters of an hour.

POTATO ROLLS.

Take five or six potatoes, boil and wash them; add salt, pepper and a little milk. Beat three eggs light and mix with them. Make out into little rolls, and cover with flour. Fry in hot lard.

Mrs. Ira Northrop.

BROILED POTATOES.

Boil eight or ten large potatoes; when cold, slice them lengthways and put on a toaster or fine wire broiler over a hot fire; when browned, remove, salt, and pour melted butter over them.

FRIED TOMATOES.

Cut the tomatoes in slices without skinning; pepper and salt them; then sprinkle a little flour over them and fry in butter until brown. Put them on a hot platter and pour milk or cream into the butter and juice. When boiling hot, pour over the tomatoes.

BAKED TOMATOES.

Skin the tomatoes, slice in small pieces; spread in bottom of a pudding dish a thick layer; cover with a thin layer of bread crumbs, and sprinkle salt, pepper and a few small pieces of butter over them; add layers of tomatoes, &c., until the dish is filled — sprinkle over the top a layer of fine rolled crackers. Bake one hour.   H. A.

BROILED TOMATOES.

Cut large tomatoes in two; crosswise; put on gridiron, cut surface down; when well seared, turn, and put butter, salt and pepper on, and cook with the skin-side down till done.

C. M.

SPICED TOMATOES.

To one pound of ripe tomatoes, peeled and sliced, add one-half pound brown sugar, one-half pint vinegar, one teaspoon cinnamon, one teaspoon allspice, one teaspoon cloves. Boil two hours.

BAKED CORN.

Grate one dozen ears sweet corn, one cup milk, small piece butter; salt, and bake in pudding dish one hour.

CORN CAKES.

One pint grated corn, two eggs, one teaspoon melted butter, three tablespoons sweet milk, two and one-half tablespoons Boston crackers, rolled. Fry in spider.

MRS. W.

CORN OYSTERS.

Eight ears of sweet corn, grated; two cups of milk, three eggs, salt and pepper; flour enough to make a batter. Put a tablespoon of butter into a frying pan and drop the mixture into the hot butter — a spoonful in a place; brown on both sides. Serve hot for breakfast or as a side dish for dinner.

MRS. SAGE.

SUCCOTASH.

Ten ears green corn, one pint Lima beans; cut the corn from the cob, and stew gently with the beans until tender. Use as little water as possible. Season with butter, salt and pepper — milk, if you choose.

EGG PLANT.

Pare and cut in slices half an inch thick; sprinkle with salt; cover and let stand for an hour. Rinse in clear cold water; wipe each slice dry; dip first in beaten egg, then in rolled cracker or bread crumbs. Season with pepper and salt, and fry brown in butter.

MRS. MILLER.

MACCARONI.

Three long sticks of maccaroni, broken in small pieces; soak in a pint of milk two hours. Grate bread and dried cheese. Put a layer of maccaroni in a pudding dish; add pepper, salt and butter; then sprinkle the bread and cheese crumbs over it, and so continue until the dish is filled. Bake until brown.

BELLE.

VEGETABLE OYSTERS.

One bunch of oysters ; boil and mash. One pint sour milk, half a teaspoon soda; flour to make a batter; add two eggs, beaten, and the oysters. Fry in hot lard — drop in spoonfuls.

C. M.

MOCK OYSTERS.

Three grated parsnips, three eggs, one teaspoon salt, one teacup sweet cream, butter half the size of an egg, three table-spoons flour. Fry as pancakes.   MRS. M. K. W.

BAKED BEANS.

One quart beans, soaked over night ; in the morning put them in a kettle with cold water and boil ten minutes ; change the water, and put with them a small piece of salt pork. Let them boil until nearly tender, then take them out of the kettle with a skimmer ; put in a baking dish, with pork in the centre ; cut the rind in small squares ; sprinkle over the top one tablespoon of white sugar ; bake three hours. If they bake dry, add the bean broth.

MRS. ADELBERT MUDGE.

BREAD.

POTATO YEAST.

Three potatoes; boil and mash them in the morning; add one-quarter cup sugar, one-half cup flour, a little salt; after stirring well, pour over one-half pint boiling water; stir and add one-half pint cold water; stir that, and add one-half cup yeast, and put it in a warm place. When it is risen well and rounds up to the top of the dish, stir it down. Do so several times during the day, and at night strain and put it in a jug. Keep in a cool place. It will be good a week.

Mrs. C. J. Baldwin.

YEAST CAKES.

Boil one-half pound of hops in eight quarts of water until the liquid is very strong; then put in fifteen or twenty large potatoes; let them boil till they are thoroughly done; take them out; pare and mash them fine. Put in the mashed potatoes a pint of flour, and strain your boiling hop liquid on to the flour and potato, taking care that the flour is well scalded. Add one pint of molasses, one tablespoonful of ginger and one handful of salt; when the mixture is cool enough to put the hand in, rub it through a colander to reduce it to a fine pulp. Add a sufficient quantity of yeast to raise it, and let it stand in a large covered jar until morning; then add another bowl of flour, and mix the cakes with Indian meal. They must be hard enough to take up a quantity of dough in the hand, pat it together and cut it into slices. Lay the cakes as you cut them on plates or something that will not impart any taste to them. The cakes must be turned once the first day, and after that twice a day until they are thoroughly dry.

Mrs. Orin Sage.

YEAST.

One handful hops, six large potatoes; boil together until well done, and strain through a colander; add sufficient water to make two quarts, and when boiling stir quickly into one quart of flour and a little salt. When lukewarm add one cup of yeast.   ELLEN.

POTATO BREAD.

Three and one-half quarts sifted flour, one boiled potato, large; one quart warm water, one teacup yeast, one even tablespoon salt. Mix at night; put the flour in a large bowl; hollow a place in the centre for the potato mashed, water and salt. Stir in flour enough to make a smooth batter; add yeast; stir in the rest of the flour. Put the dough on the floured board; knead fifteen minutes, using barely enough flour to prevent sticking. Flour the bowl, lay the dough in it, cover, and leave to rise. In the morning, divide in four parts; mould into loaves; when light, prick, and bake in a moderate oven.

SALT RAISING BREAD.

Pour a pint of hot water in a two-quart pail or pitcher on one-half tablespoon of salt; when the finger can be held in it, add one and one-third pints of flour; mix well, and leave the pitcher in a kettle of water, as warm as that used in mixing. Keep it at the same temperature until the batter is nearly twice its original bulk (which will be in from five to eight hours). It may be stirred once or twice during the rising. Add to this a sponge made of one quart of hot water, two and one-half quarts of flour — adding as much more as may be necessary to make a soft dough; mix well, and leave in a warm place to rise. When light, mould into loaves, keeping them as soft as possible; lay in buttered tins. When light again, prick, and bake.

BREAD.

Five quarts flour, one tablespoon salt, two quarts lukewarm water, one cup of yeast. Knead thoroughly, and leave in warm place all night. In the morning make into five loaves, and when light bake one hour. ELLEN.

BISCUIT.

Two quarts flour (full) ; one quart milk or water, one cup lard, one-half cup yeast, one tablespoon sugar, salt. Melt the lard in half the milk (or water) ; when it comes to a boil, pour on the flour, thoroughly scalding the quantity it will wet ; then put in the remaining milk, cold; add the other ingredients ; mould thoroughly, like bread, and let stand to rise very light (which will take from five to six hours) ; then stir down, and put where it will be cold. As fast as it rises, work it down, until entirely cold ; then mould it, and leave where it will be cold as possible without freezing. This dough will keep a week, and when wanted can be rolled, cut, and baked like soda biscuit — letting them stand to rise ten minutes on the pans before baking. MRS. A. A. MORGAN.

FRENCH ROLLS.

One pint of milk, scalded ; put into it while hot half a cup of sugar and one tablespoon of butter ; when the milk is cool, add a little salt and half a cup of yeast, or one compressed yeast cake; stir in flour to make a stiff sponge, and when light mix as for bread. Let it rise until light, punch it down with the hand, and let it rise again — repeat two or three times ; then turn the dough on to the moulding board, and pound with the rolling-pin until thin enough to cut. Cut out with a tumbler, brush the surface of each one with melted butter, and fold over. Let the rolls rise on the tins ; bake, and while warm brush over the surface with melted butter to make the crust tender. MRS. W. N. S.

PARKER HOUSE ROLLS.

One teacup home made yeast, a little salt, one tablespoon sugar, piece of lard size of an egg, one pint milk, flour sufficient to mix. Put the milk on the stove to scald with the lard in it. Prepare the flour with salt, sugar and yeast. Then add the milk, not too hot. Knead thoroughly when mixed at night; in the morning but very slight kneading is necessary. Then roll out and cut with large biscuit cutter. Spread a little butter on each roll and lap together. Let them rise very light, then bake in a quick oven.

MRS. E. FOSTER HOYT.

PARKER HOUSE ROLLS.

One quart flour, one ounce lard, one-half pint milk, one-half gill yeast, one-half tablespoon sugar, one-half teaspoon salt. In the evening put the flour in a bowl; put the salt and lard in the milk, and warm until the lard is melted. When the milk is lukewarm, add the yeast; mix well, and pour into the centre of the flour. Do not stir it. Cover and leave it in the cellar. In the morning work it thoroughly and let rise; two hours before tea, roll it out two-thirds of an inch thick; cut with a tin cutter four inches across. With a feather coat half of the top with melted butter, and lap it nearly over the other half. Then draw them out a little, to make them roll-shaped; lay them apart in buttered pans, and when light bake.

MRS. MILLER.

RUSK.

Four eggs, two cups sugar, one cup butter, one pint milk, three-fourths cup yeast. Beat eggs and sugar together, and mix all soft with flour. Let them rise over night; mix again, and when light make into biscuit; put in tins, and raise again before baking.

When taken from the oven, rub the top with sugar and and cream.

MRS. WOODBURY.

TEA RUSK.

Three cups of flour, one cup of milk, three-fourths cup of sugar, two heaping tablespoons of butter, melted ; two eggs, three teaspoons baking powder.

MRS. W. L. SAGE.

BROWN BREAD.

Three cups corn meal, two cups brown flour, one cup molasses, little salt, one teaspoon saleratus, three and one-half cups warm water. Steam two and one-half hours.

MRS. M. K. W.

RYE BREAD.

One pint rye meal, one pint Indian meal, one cup molasses, one teaspoon saleratus, one teaspoon salt, two cups sour milk. Mix the rye, Indian, salt and saleratus together ; put in the molasses and mix with the milk. Steam four hours.

MRS. WOODBURY.

BROWN BREAD.

One quart of sour milk, one-half cup of molasses, one-half cup of sugar, two eggs, three tablespoons of melted butter, one teaspoon of soda. Mix with brown flour as stiff as you can stir it with a spoon.

To make gems or puffs for breakfast, use a little less flour, and bake in muffin rings or gem pans.

BOSTON BROWN BREAD.

One and one-half pints Indian meal, one and one-half pints rye meal, one cup molasses, two tablespoons vinegar, one teaspoon salt, two teaspoons saleratus, one quart luke-warm water. Boil or bake five hours.

MRS. E. W. SAGE.

GRAHAM BREAD.

One bowl soft bread sponge, one-half cup brown sugar, three tablespoons butter, very little soda. Dissolve in warm water; stir to a thick batter with Graham flour; put in tins, and let rise until very light; then bake.

MRS. B. N. HURD.

CORN BREAD.

One quart Indian meal, one pint Graham flour, one pint sweet milk, one pint of butter or sour milk, one-half teacup of molasses, one full teaspoon of soda. Steam three hours.

MRS. EDWIN O. SAGE.

CORN BREAD.

One pint corn meal, one pint bread sponge, two-thirds cup molasses, one teaspoon soda. Scald the meal; when cool add the sponge, molasses and soda. Mix with Graham flour stiff as cake; put in tins, and when light bake one hour.

SENECA POINT.

JOHNNY CAKE.

Two eggs, three cups butter-milk or sour milk, one-half cup lard, one-half cup sugar, one cup flour, one teaspoon saleratus, one-half teaspoon salt, three cups Indian meal.

MRS. H. E. B.

BAKING POWDER BISCUIT.

One quart flour, four teaspoons baking powder, a little salt — sifted together; add a full teaspoon of butter and sufficient water to make soft dough. Roll out, and cut in cakes an inch thick. Bake in quick oven. ELLEN.

TEA PUFFS.

Two and one-quarter cups flour, three cups milk, three eggs — whites and yolks beaten separately; three teaspoons melted butter, a little salt. Bake in cups, in a hot oven.

MRS. GEO. DARLING.

INDIAN CORN MUFFINS.

Beat one egg thoroughly; put in a coffee-cup; add one tablespoon brown sugar, one tablespoon thick cream or butter; fill with butter-milk or sour milk, two handfuls corn meal, one small handful wheat flour, one-half teaspoon soda — rubbed into the flour. Bake in muffin rings on a griddle.

MRS. EDWIN PANCOST.

MUFFINS.

One cup of home-made yeast or half of a compressed yeast cake, one pint of sweet milk, two eggs, two tablespoons of melted butter, two tablespoons of sugar. Beat the butter, sugar and eggs well together; then stir in the milk, slightly warmed, and thicken with flour to the consistency of griddle cakes. When light, bake in muffin rings or on a griddle.

Muffins should never be cut with a knife, but be pulled open with the fingers.

If wanted for tea, the batter must be mixed immediately after breakfast. MRS. S.

MUFFINS.

Three pints flour, one quart milk, two eggs, four teaspoons baking powder, one teaspoon salt (one teaspoon butter, one teaspoon lard — melt together). Bake in quick oven.

BREAKFAST PUFFS.

Four eggs, four cups milk, four cups flour. Beat milk, yolks of egg and flour together; add the whites beaten stiff. Bake in quick oven, in gem irons.

MRS. E. F. WILSON.

GEMS.

One pint warm water, one teaspoon salt, Graham flour enough to make stiff batter. Have your irons and oven both hot.

GRAHAM PUFFS.

One quart of Graham flour, one pint of milk, one pint of water, two eggs, a little salt. Bake in cups or gem pans.

HUCKLEBERRY CAKE.

One cup of sugar, one cup of milk, two and one-half cups of flour, one egg, butter the size of an egg, two teaspoons of baking powder, one and one-half cups of huckleberries. To be eaten hot with butter. This makes a very delicate tea rusk by leaving out the huckleberries, and using only half a cup of sugar.   MRS. SAGE.

SHORT CAKE.

Three teaspoons baking powder, sifted with one and one-half pints flour; three tablespoons butter, rubbed into the flour; one-half cup sugar; teaspoon salt; one egg, beaten with one pint milk. Bake in jelly tins. Spread with butter, and put berries between layers.

MATTIE C. DAYFOOT.

DEMOCRATS.

One-half cup of sugar, one-quarter cup butter, one cup sweet milk, one pint flour, three eggs, two and one-half teaspoons baking powder. Bake in cups for tea.

MRS. J. M. P.

RICE GRIDDLE CAKES.

For a small quantity, say one quart bowl full, take one egg, two-thirds of rice (cooked) to one-third flour; one teaspoon soda, two teaspoons cream tartar, or three teaspoons baking powder; sweet milk enough to make it the right consistency.   MRS. OREN SAGE.

WHEAT CAKES.

One pint sour milk, teaspoon soda, a little salt, two eggs, flour to make a thin batter.

WAFFLES.

If you want your waffles for tea, take one quart warm milk after dinner; put in two eggs, beaten; a small piece of butter; a small cup of yeast. Mix with flour a little thicker than wheat pancakes. Set by warm stove and they will be light for tea. Baked in waffle irons, greased.

Mrs. J. H. Hurd.

WAFFLES.

Three eggs, one quart sour milk, one teaspoon soda, a little salt, two tablespoons melted butter. Beat the yolks thoroughly; stir in the milk, butter and soda, lastly the whites, beaten stiff. Use flour to make stiffer than pancakes. Bake in waffle irons. Serve with butter and sugar.

EGG TOAST.

For six persons, take two eggs, one-half cup milk, flour enough to make a good stiff batter. Cut old bread in thin slices; dip into the batter, and fry brown in butter. Serve hot.

Mrs. L.

PIES.

PIE CRUST.

One-half cup lard, one-half cup butter, one quart sifted flour, one cup cold water, a little salt. Rub the butter and lard *slightly* into the flour; wet it with the water, mixing it as little as possible.

This quantity will make two large or three small pies.

MRS. W. N. SAGE.

PIE CRUST GLAZE.

To prevent the juice from soaking the under crust, beat up the white of an egg, and before filling the pie, brush over the crust with the beaten egg. Brush over the top crust also, to give it a beautiful yellow brown.

CUSTARD PIE.

One pint of milk, three eggs, a little salt, three tablespoons of sugar. Flavor with vanilla or nutmeg and essence of lemon. If the milk is scalded, it will require but two eggs to a pint.

COCOANUT PIE.

Make a custard and add a small cup of cocoanut.

RICE PIE.

For two pies, take two tablespoons of rice; wash and put it into a farina boiler with a quart of milk; cook until perfectly soft. Let it cool; add three eggs, well beaten, with three tablespoons of sugar and one of butter; a little salt, cinnamon and a few stoned raisins. Bake with under crust.

MRS. W. N. S.

CREAM PIE.

One pint of milk, scalded; two tablespoons of corn starch, three tablespoons of sugar, yolks of two eggs. Wet the starch with a little cold milk; beat the eggs and sugar until light, and stir the whole into the scalding milk. Flavor with lemon or vanilla, and set aside to cool. Line a plate with pie crust and bake; fill it with cream, and cover it with frosting made of the whites of the eggs, beaten dry, with two tablespoons of sugar. Bake a delicate brown.

MRS. EDWIN PANCOST.

CREAM PIE ELEGANTE.

For one pie, beat together one cup sugar, one-half cup corn starch, two eggs. Stir into one pint hot milk; when well cooked and cool, flavor and put between crusts which have been baked and are cold.

CRUST FOR PIE.

One pint flour, one-half teacup lard, one-quarter teacup ice water, teaspoon salt. Bake upper and lower crusts in separate plates, and put the cream between.

PLAIN APPLE PIE.

Line your plate with pastry; fill with sliced sour apples; cover with crust without pressing down the outer edge. Bake light brown, and when done remove the upper crust, and season with butter, sugar and spice to taste.

LINCOLN PIE.

One pint stewed sour apples, sifted; butter size of an egg, two tablespoons flour; grated rind and juice of a lemon; yolks of three eggs, beaten. Sweeten to taste. Bake with lower crust, and when done spread a meringue of the whites of three eggs, beaten with three tablespoons sugar over the top, and brown in oven.

MRS. M. K. W.

PUMPKIN PIE.

One quart pumpkin, three pints milk, three or four eggs. Spice and sweeten to taste. A little salt.   C. M.

PUMPKIN PIE.

One cup stewed pumpkin, one coffeecup milk, three eggs, piece of butter size of a walnut, two teaspoons cinnamon, one teaspoon ginger, a little salt and pepper. Sweeten with molasses.   MRS. SUGRU.

SQUASH PIE.

One full cup stewed squash, one scant cup sugar, one pint milk, two eggs, two tablespoons melted butter, a little salt, ginger and cinnamon.   MRS. W. N. S.

PIE PLANT PIE.

Two cups pie plant, one tablespoon water, one-half cup sugar, a little butter. Crust: one pint flour, one-half cup lard; pinch salt; water to roll out.

PORK PIE.

Cover the dish with crust; put layer of apples, sliced thin; a layer of pork (salt and raw), sliced very thin and in small pieces. Black pepper and spices to taste. Sugar upper crust. Bake one hour and a half.

COCOANUT PIE.

One cup powdered sugar, one-half cup butter, four eggs, one cup grated cocoanut, one quart milk. Put the cocoanut with the butter and sugar; add the milk and eggs. Makes two pies.   BUFFALO.

COCOANUT PIE.

One cup sugar, one-half cup butter, one-half grated cocoanut, one quart milk, four eggs, one teaspoon corn starch. Beat sugar and butter together; add the eggs, then the cocoanut, lastly the milk. This will make two pies.

MRS. HATTIE GILBERT.

A VERY RICH LEMON PIE.

One large lemon, one teaspoon of butter (heaping); one and one-half cups of sugar, three eggs, one heaping teaspoon of flour, one-half glass of brandy. Grate the yellow part of the rind and squeeze the juice of the lemon; beat the butter and sugar to a cream with the yolks of the eggs; then stir in the grated rind and juice, flour and brandy; lastly whip and stir in the whites. Bake with an under crust.

LEMON PIE.

One cup sugar; yolks of three eggs, stirred to cream; add tablespoon flour; grated rind and juice of two lemons; one coffeecup milk. Bake with under crust. Make a meringue of whites of the eggs and three tablespoons of sugar; spread over the top of pie. Set in oven and brown slightly.

E. I. G.

CHOCOLATE PIE.

One coffeecup milk, two tablespoons grated chocolate, three-fourths cup sugar, yolks three eggs. Heat chocolate and milk together; add the sugar and yolks together, beaten to cream. Flavor with vanilla. Bake with under crust. Spread meringue of the whites over the top.

ELLA I. GOULD.

RICH MINCE PIES.

Four pounds of meat, two pounds of suet, eight pounds of apples, six pounds of sugar, four and one-half pounds of raisins (stoned); one pint of brandy; ten nutmegs; add cinnamon, cloves, salt and citron to your taste. Wet with boiled cider. This quantity will make twenty-four pies on the largest sized plates.

MINCE MEAT FOR PIES.

Four pounds of round of beef, seven pounds apples, five pounds raisins (chopped or stoned); two pounds suet, seven pounds sugar, one pint brandy, ten nutmegs, grated; cinnamon and cloves to taste; a little salt, three-fourths pound citron, sliced fine. Boil beef until tender; when cold chop fine, add the apples, chopped also, and the other ingredients. This quantity makes a three gallon crock full.

MRS. A. S. LANE.

MINCE PIES. (Makes 17).

Boil one large or two small beef hearts; one and one-half pounds fine chopped suet, six pints fine chopped sour apples, two pounds fine chopped raisins, two pounds currants, one pound fine chopped citron, one quart molasses, two pounds brown sugar, one quart brandy, two quarts cider, one ounce allspice, one ounce cinnamon, three nutmegs. Chop the meat when cold, add the other ingredients and cook one hour; let it stand two days before making into pies, then if too rich add more apples.

MOCK MINCE PIE.

Two cups sugar, one small cup butter, one-half cup of molasses, two eggs, one cup rolled crackers, one cup cold water, one cup wine, one-half cup boiled cider, one cup chopped raisins, a little salt, cinnamon and cloves.

MRS. SAGE.

PLAIN AND FANCY DESSERTS.

GENERAL DIRECTIONS.

FLOUR. — Should always be sifted just before you wish to use it.

CREAM OF TARTAR, OR BAKING POWDER — Should be thoroughly mixed with the flour.

SODA — Should always be dissolved in the milk.

BUTTER AND SUGAR FOR CAKE — Should always be beaten to a cream.

EGGS — Beat the yolks until you can take up a spoon *full;* whip the whites to a stiff froth and stir them into the cake with the flour the last thing before putting the flour into the tins.

TO BOIL A PUDDING IN A BAG — Dip the bag (which should be made of thick cotton or linen) in hot water, and rub the inside with flour before putting in the pudding; when done, dip the bag in cold water and the pudding will turn out easily. Always put a plate on the bottom of the kettle to keep the pudding from burning.

TO STEAM A PUDDING — Put it into a tin pan or earthen dish, tie a cloth over the top and set it into a steamer, cover the steamer closely; allow a little longer time than you do for boiling. MRS. W. N. SAGE.

WEIGHTS AND MEASURES.

Two cups of sifted flour weighs . . .	one pound.
One pint sifted flour weighs	one pound.
One pint white sugar weighs . . .	one pound.
Two tablespoons of liquid	one ounce.
Eight teaspoons of liquid . .	one ounce.
One gill of liquid . . ˙ . . .	four ounces.
One pint of liquid	sixteen ounces.

MRS. W. N. SAGE.

SUET PUDDING.

One cup suet or butter, one cup molasses, one bowl of raisins and currants, one egg, one cup sweet milk, one teaspoon saleratus, dissolved in milk ; one-fourth teaspoon cloves, one-half nutmeg.   Mix stiff with flour and steam three hours.

SAUCE.

One cup butter and two cups sugar, beat to a cream ; add three eggs beaten very light ; stir in two tablespoons boiling water.   Flavor with wine, brandy, or vanilla.

Mrs. M. B. B.

PLUM PUDDING.

One pound raisins, stoned ; one pound currants, three-fourths pound suet, chopped fine ; three eggs, one coffeecup sugar, one teaspoon soda, a little nutmeg and salt ; moisten with milk, and add flour to mix soft.   Tie in a bag, leaving room to swell, and boil from three to four hours.   Serve with sauce.   Mrs. A. S. LANE.

ENGLISH PLUM PUDDING.

Two pounds suet, chopped ; three pounds raisins, seeded ; two pounds currants, one-half pound citron, two pounds sugar, five eggs, one pint milk, one-half pint brandy, two or three nutmegs, a little salt, flour to make very stiff.   Put in one or two bags, and boil in a large quantity of water seven or eight hours.   Serve with sauce.

Mrs. A. S. LANE.

GRAHAM PUDDING.

One and one-half cups Graham flour, one-half cup molasses, one-fourth cup melted butter, one-half cup sweet milk, one egg, even teaspoon soda, little salt, one-half cup raisins, one-half cup currants, one teaspoon cloves, one teaspoon cinnamon, one-fourth of a nutmeg.   Steam two and one-half hours. Serve with warm sauce.   Mrs. WOODBURY.

SWEET POTATO PUDDING.

One-half dozen good sized potatoes, grated raw ; one table-spoon of butter, one tablespoon of lard, one pint molasses, three tablespoons brown sugar, one-half pint milk, one egg, one teaspoon cloves, allspice and ginger, two teaspoons salt, water to make a soft batter. Stir two or three times while baking. Bake slow for two hours.

MRS. BATTELLE.

APPLE PUDDING.

Fill a dish with apples nicely sliced, sweeten them, add spices, nutmeg, a little lemon or vanilla, and cover with a crust ; set on top of the stove until the crust rises, then bake a nice brown.

CRUST.

One quart flour, three teaspoons baking powder, piece of butter size of an egg, salt, milk enough to mix soft dough.

SAUCE FOR ABOVE.

One egg, one cup fine sugar, beaten very light ; pour a little boiling water over until the consistency of cream. Flavor with vanilla, and grate a little nutmeg on top.

MISS FOSDICK.

BREAD PUDDING.

One pint bread crumbs, one quart milk, rind of one lemon grated into milk ; yolks four eggs, beaten and mixed with one-half cup sugar. Bake one-half hour. Spread meringue on top. MRS. PITKIN.

STEAMED PUDDING.

One egg, one large teacup sour milk, a little cream or butter, one teaspoon soda. Mix soft and put in deep pie plates or a pudding dish. Fill with blackberries or other pressed fruits. Steam one hour, and serve with sweetened cream, or sauce. MARY.

QUAKER PUDDING.

Six eggs, beaten with nine or ten tablespoons flour and quart milk. Bake about twenty minutes. Serve with sauce.

GRANDMA B.

RICE PUDDING.

One teacup rice, one teacup sugar, one teacup raisins, small piece butter, a little salt, two quarts milk. Bake from an hour and a half to two hours. Serve with sauce.

QUEEN'S PUDDING.

One pint of bread crumbs, one quart of milk, warmed and poured over the crumbs; yolks of four eggs, well beaten with one cup of sugar and one teaspoon of butter. When baked, spread over the top a layer of jelly or preserves. Beat the whites of the eggs dry, and add two tablespoons of sugar and spread over the top. Bake a light brown. Serve warm with sauce, or cold with sugar and cream.

ANGELS' FOOD.

Dissolve one-half box of gelatine in one quart of milk; beat together the yolks of three eggs; one cup of sugar, and the juice of one lemon; stir it into the gelatine and milk, and let it just come to a boil; flavor with vanilla. When nearly cold, whip the whites of the eggs to a stiff froth, and stir through the custard. Pour into moulds and set away to cool.

COTTAGE PUDDING.

Two tablespoons melted butter, one cup sugar, three small cups flour, one cup milk, one egg, three teaspoons baking powder.

POOR MAN'S PUDDING.

One-half cup of rice washed thoroughly; three-fourths cup of sugar, one teaspoon cinnamon, one and one-half quarts sweet milk. Stir occasionally; add milk as it boils away, until it is the consistency of thick cream, and quite brown.

MRS. W. T. MILLS.

BROWN BETTIE.

One-third of bread and two-thirds of apples. Crumb the bread fine and chop the apples; two cups of brown sugar, one-half cup butter, two teaspoons of cinnamon, little nutmeg. Mix thoroughly and spread over the apples and bread. Bake very brown.

SAUCE.

One teaspoon butter, one-half cup brown sugar, one pint boiling water, one teaspoon of flour; flavor with vanilla or wine.

MRS. C. F. PAINE.

INDIAN PUDDING.

Add to one quart boiling milk two well beaten eggs; three tablespoons Indian meal, one tablespoon flour, a little salt. Bake three-quarters of an hour. Serve with sugar and cream.

MRS. A. A. MORGAN.

APPLE DUMPLINGS.

Fill a dish two-thirds full of apples, pared and quartered; cover with biscuit-crust one-half inch thick. Steam one-half hour.

BOILED CUSTARD.

Six eggs, one quart milk, six tablespoons; sugar scald milk, add the sugar and eggs beaten together. Stir until done.

BAKED CUSTARD.

One quart milk, four well-beaten eggs, four tablespoons sugar. Flavor to taste. Bake in moderate oven.

TAPIOCA PUDDING.

One small cup of tapioca, one quart of milk, one teaspoon of butter, three tablespoons of sugar. Soak the tapioca in water four or five hours, then add the milk; flavor with essence of lemon or anything else you prefer. Bake slowly one hour. To be made the day before it is wanted, and eaten cold with cream or milk and sugar. Some prefer the pudding made with three pints of milk and no water.

APPLE TAPIOCA PUDDING.

Pare and core enough apples to fill a dish; put into each apple a bit of lemon peel. Soak half a pint of tapioca in one quart of lukewarm water one hour; add a little salt; flavor with lemon; pour over the apples. Bake until apples are tender. Eat when cold, with cream and sugar.

TAPIOCA AND COCOANUT PUDDING.

One cup tapioca, soaked over night; one quart milk, yolks of four eggs, white of two, one cup sugar, two tablespoons grated cocoanut. Bake one-half hour. Make frosting of whites two eggs, three tablespoons sugar, two tablespoons grated cocoanut; spread over the pudding when baked. Set in the oven until a light brown.

DELIA.

TAPIOCA CREAM.

Three tablespoons tapioca, soaked in a teacup of water over night; add one quart of milk; stir together and boil twenty minutes. Beat the yolks of three eggs and one cup sugar thoroughly; stir into the milk; flavor with vanilla. Beat the whites very stiff, put in the bottom of the dish and pour the rest over it. Serve cold.

PUFFS.

Two cups flour, two teaspoons baking powder sifted together; add one and three-fourths cups sweet milk, one teaspoon melted butter, one-half cup sugar, one egg; stir quickly. Bake in patty tins twenty minutes.   Serve with sauce.

Mrs. H. C.

FRITTERS.

Two cups flour, two teaspoons baking powder, two eggs, milk enough for stiff batter, a little salt.   Drop into boiling lard; fry light brown.   Serve with cream and sugar or sauce.

FRITTERS.

One cup sour milk, one egg, one-half teaspoon salt; flour to make stiff batter; one even teaspoon soda — last thing. Fry in lard.   To be eaten with lemon and sugar, or cider sweetened and hot.

E. B.

TAPIOCA MERINGUE.

One small cup of tapioca, three pints of milk, three eggs. Soak the tapioca in the milk two hours or more; cook in a farina boiler until soft; beat the yolks of the eggs and stir in. Sweeten, flavor and set away to cool.   Before sending to table, whip the whites to a stiff froth and stir in lightly.

Mrs. W. N. S.

RICE MERINGUE.

One-half tea cup of rice, one quart of milk, four eggs, eight teaspoons of fine sugar, a little salt.   Boil the rice in the milk until it is soft; beat the yolks of the eggs with four spoons of the sugar and stir into the rice while it is hot. Flavor with vanilla, and put the mixture into your pudding dish.   Beat the whites of the eggs dry; stir in the other four spoons of sugar; spread the frosting evenly over the pudding and bake a light brown.

Mrs. W. N. S.

CAKE MERINGUE.

Line a pudding dish with cake; fill it with boiled custard; spread a meringue over the top, and bake a light brown.

Mrs. A. S. Mann.

COCOANUT PUDDING.

One pint rich milk, two tablespoons corn starch, whites of four eggs, scant half cup sugar, a little salt. Put the milk over the fire, and when boiling add the corn starch, wet with a little cold milk ; then the sugar, stirring constantly, until it makes a smooth paste. Then take from the fire and stir in the beaten eggs. Flavor with lemon or vanilla, and when slightly cooled add half a grated cocoanut. Pour into a mould; set in a cold place. Serve with soft custard.

Miss Morgan.

COCOANUT PUDDING.

One-half pound sugar, one quarter pound butter, one-half pound grated cocoanut, whites of three eggs ; one tablespoon rose-water, two tablespoons cherry wine. Beat the sugar and butter to a cream; beat whites until stiff and add to the butter and sugar. Add the cocoanut last. Bake and serve with sauce.

Mrs. E. H.

CHOCOLATE PUDDING.

One quart of milk, scalded ; one and one-half squares of chocolate, grated ; wet with cold milk, and stir into the scalded milk. When the chocolate is dissolved, pour into a pudding dish ; add the yolks of six eggs, well beaten, and six tablespoons sugar. Bake about three-quarters of an hour. Beat the whites of the eggs to stiff froth ; add six tablespoons sugar. Spread the frosting over the top ; set again in the oven until a light brown.

Mrs. E. W. Sage.

SPONGE PUDDING.

One small stale sponge cake, one coffeecup seeded raisins, one-quarter cup currants, one quart milk, three eggs. Must have a tin mould with a chimney. Butter the mould well; flatten the raisins, and put thick on the mould. Crumb the cake in the mould with the currants. Mix the eggs and milk as for a custard, and pour in the mould; cover tight and boil three-quarters of an hour; then put it on a platter, and set in the oven for a few minutes.

For sauce, make a thin boiled custard.

MRS. GEO. DARLING.

SPONGE PUDDING.

One heaping coffeecup of flour, stirred perfectly smooth in one quart of milk. Set in boiling water and stir constantly until flour is well cooked. When nearly cold, add two teaspoons melted butter, one small teacup sugar, yolk twelve eggs (beaten to froth) — mix together. Just before baking, add the whites of twelve eggs, well beaten. Have in oven a dripping pan half full of boiling water; put the pudding in buttered tin dish, and set in dripping pan. Bake in moderate oven three-quarters of an hour. Serve with sugar and cream or sauce. SYRACUSE.

ORANGE SPONGE PUDDING.

Cut five or six oranges in small pieces and place in a pudding dish; pour over them one coffeecup sugar; then make a boiled custard of one pint milk, yolks of three eggs, one-half cup sugar, one large teaspoon corn starch; pour this over the oranges. Make a meringue of the beaten whites of the eggs with three tablespoons of powdered sugar, and put over the top of the pudding, and brown it slightly in the oven.

EMMA SATTERLEE.

ECLAIR PUDDING.

Four eggs, one cup sugar, one cup flour, one teaspoon vanilla, one teaspoon baking powder. When baked spread the top with chocolate icing.

ICING.

White of one egg, one-half teacup milk, one-half teacup sugar, four tablespoons grated chocolate; boil until thick and smooth. Just before serving the pudding split and fill with the following:

CUSTARD.

One pint of milk, a little salt, yolks of three eggs, one-half cup sugar, two tablespoons corn starch; flavor with vanilla and lemon.   IDA M. SATTERLEE.

DELMONICO PUDDING.

One quart of milk, four eggs (leave out the whites of three); three tablespoons of sugar, two tablespoons of corn starch, one cup of cocoanut, a little salt. Put the milk in a farina boiler to scald; wet the starch in cold milk; beat the eggs and sugar, and stir all into the scalding milk; add the cocoanut, and pour the whole into a pudding dish; whip the three whites dry with three tablespoons of sugar; flavor with lemon or vanilla; spread over the pudding and bake a light brown. Eat hot or cold.

                                        MRS. W. N. S.

ORANGE PUDDING.

Four sweet oranges, sliced small; one quart milk, one cup sugar, two tablespoons corn starch, yolks of three eggs. Heat the milk, when nearly boiling add the corn starch (wet with a little cold milk), the sugar and eggs, thoroughly beaten. Boil until thick as custard; when cold pour over the sliced oranges. Make a meringue of the whites of three eggs and one small teacup of sugar; spread on pudding, and put sliced oranges on top of this.   E. I. G.

PORCUPINE PUDDING.

One cup sugar, one cup flour, three eggs, three teaspoons baking powder, dissolved in teaspoon of milk; bake in a round tin. Frost cake, top and sides, thickly; stick blanched almonds over top of cake with points up; make floating island; put cake on glass standard; pour a little custard with snow around the edge of standard; on each spot of snow drop a little jelly; use rest of custard as sauce.

Mrs. H. C.

SNOW PUDDING.

One-half box gelatine, soaked in cup of water one hour; two lemons, grated; three eggs, one and one-half cups sugar. Add sugar and lemons to gelatine, then pour over one-half pint boiling water. When dissolved beat until all sparkles; then add the whites of eggs beaten stiff. Make a custard of yolks.

Ella.

PUDDING SAUCE.

One tablespoon flour, butter size of an egg, one-half pint sugar, grated peel and juice of one or two lemons, to suit taste; mix flour and butter together, then add sugar and lemon; then put into one-half pint boiling water, boil until it thickens, cool a little, then add well beaten egg.

M. C.

FOAM SAUCE.

One cup pulverized sugar, two eggs; beat sugar and yolks together in a bowl; set in boiling water; stir until hot; then add whites beaten stiff. Put a small piece of butter and tablespoon of brandy in a dish: pour over them the sugar and eggs just before serving.

Ella I. G.

PUDDING SAUCE.

One cup sugar, two eggs; beat the yolks very light, add sugar, mix thoroughly, add the whites, beaten to a stiff froth; then add two tablespoons brandy. Serve as soon as made.

E. B. P.

PUDDING SAUCE (Cold).

One heaping tablespoon of butter, one cup of fine sugar, one glass of sherry or Madeira wine. Beat the butter and sugar to a cream, and gradually beat in the wine; grate a little nutmeg over it before sending to table.

MRS. W. N. S.

WINE SAUCE (Hot).

Boil one-half pint of water with a tablespoon of flour, and strain on the sauce made as above just before sending it to table. Set it over the top of the tea-kettle three or four minutes.   MRS. W. N. S.

CHOCOLATE BLANC MANGE.

One quart of milk, one-half box gelatine, soaked in one cup water; four tablespoons grated chocolate, rubbed smooth in a little milk; three eggs, vanilla. Heat the milk until boiling, then add the other ingredients; boil five minutes, pour into mould. Serve cold with sugar and cream, or custard.   ELLA I. GOULD.

CORN STARCH BLANC MANGE.

One quart milk, one cup sugar, three tablespoons corn starch; flavor with lemon or vanilla. Boil the milk and sugar together, flavor, then stir in corn starch dissolved in a little cold milk. Boil and turn into mould.

MRS. GILBERT.

CARAMEL CUSTARD.

Put two dessert spoons of crushed sugar in a tin pan. Let it stand on the stove until it begins to brown, then stir constantly until it is a thick, black syrup. Pour it into a quart of scalding milk; add six ounces of white sugar and the yolks of six eggs. Beat and pour into cups, set in a pan of hot water in the oven, and bake twenty minutes.

MRS. M. K. W.

APPLE SNOW.

Mash the pulp of three baked apples with silver spoon; add one cup sugar, and the beaten white of an egg; flavor and beat one-half hour. Serve on soft custard or alone.

JENNIE MORGAN.

SNOW DRIFT.

Two strips (or one-half ounce) işinglass, soaked in cold water twenty or thirty minutes. Take it from the cold water and pour over it one pint boiling water; add two cups granulated sugar and the juice of two lemons. Put it on the ice, and when thick beat into the beaten whites of four eggs. Then put in mould and place on ice. Serve with boiled custard.

MRS. M. K. W.

CHARLOTTE RUSSE ELEGANTE.

One-half package Coxe's gelatine dissolved in a very little water; one quart whipped cream; flavored and sweetened to taste. Line a mould with sponge or white cake. Stir the gelatine into the cream and pour into the prepared mould. The cake may be soaked in a little wine if preferred.

MRS. H. CANDEE.

CHARLOTTE RUSSE.

Two tablespoons gelatine soaked in a little cold milk two hours; two coffeecups rich cream; one teacup milk. Whip the cream stiff in a large bowl or dish; set on ice. Boil the milk and pour gradually over the gelatine until dissolved, then strain; when nearly cold add the whipped cream, a spoonful at a time. Sweeten with pulverized sugar, and flavor with vanilla. Line a dish with lady fingers or sponge cake; pour in the cream and set in a cool place to harden.

ELLA I. GOULD.

SPANISH CREAM.

Make a soft custard of one quart milk, yolks of six eggs, six tablespoons sugar. Put one box gelatine dissolved in one-half pint water over the fire; add the custard; flavor with vanilla. Strain into moulds. Set in cool place.

DELIA.

RUSSE CREAM.

One-half box gelatine, soaked in a little water one-half hour; one quart milk, one cup sugar, four eggs. Mix sugar, milk, yolks of eggs and gelatine together; put in a pail set in a kettle of water, and boil twenty minutes. Beat the whites of the eggs stiff and stir into custard after taking off the fire. Flavor with vanilla, and pour into moulds. Serve with sugar and cream or custard.

WHIPPED CREAM.

To one quart cream whipped very thick, add powdered sugar to taste; then one tumbler of wine. Make just before ready to use. MRS. W. C. R.

SNOW JELLY.

One-half box gelatine covered with cold water. Let it stand while mixing. Two cups sugar, juice two lemons, whites of three eggs beaten stiff. Add to gelatine one pint boiling water, the sugar and eggs; beat thoroughly and strain into moulds. Make a custard of one pint milk, three eggs' yolk; turn over the jelly just before serving.

MRS. LANE.

WINE JELLY.

One-half box Coxe's gelatine, soaked in one-half pint cold water one hour; add one pint boiling water, two cups sugar, two lemons, grated; two-thirds pint sherry wine. Let all come to to a boil, then strain into moulds and set in a cool place to harden. A. H.

LEMON JELLY.

One-half box Coxe's gelatine, soaked in one-half pint cold water one hour; add one pint boiling water, and one and one-half cups sugar, three lemons, grated. Stand on stove until boiling. Strain into a mould and set in cool place.

CIDER JELLY.

One box gelatine dissolved in one pint cold water. In twenty minutes add one pint boiling water, then one quart cider and one pint sugar (granulated), and the grated rind and juice of two lemons. Let it stand on the stove until hot, but not boil. Then strain into moulds.

MRS. E. S. CONVERSE.

CAKE.

SOFT GINGERBREAD.

One-half cup butter, two cups molasses, one cup sugar, four cups flour, one cup sour milk, four eggs, one teaspoon saleratus, ginger and cloves. M. C.

GINGERBREAD.

One cup brown sugar, and one tablespoon butter, stirred to a cream; add one cup New Orleans molasses, and mix well; then add one cup sour milk, one teaspoon soda dissolved in a little of the sour milk. Mix all together, and stir in two and a half cups flour; put in ginger or spice to taste. Bake in one large loaf one hour, or two small loaves one-half hour.

ELLEN.

GINGERBREAD.

One cup brown sugar, one cup molasses, three-fourths cup butter, one teaspoon cinnamon, two teaspoons ginger. Stir together and put on the stove and warm, while sifting flour and beating the eggs. Then add one teacup sour milk, two eggs, four and one-half cups flour, one teaspoon soda, dissolved in a little hot water. Put in after the sour milk, one teacup chopped raisins.   MRS. E. HOLMES.

GINGER COOKIES.

One cup molasses, one-half cup lard, one-half cup boiling water, one teaspoon soda, one teaspoon ginger, a little salt, flour to roll out.

SEED COOKIES.

Two small cups of sugar, one cup butter, one-half cup sweet milk, one egg, two teaspoons baking powder, caraway seed. Mix very soft, roll out, cut in shapes; sprinkle sugar over the top and bake.   MRS. G. GOULD.

MOLASSES COOKIES.

One cup butter, one cup brown sugar, one cup New Orleans molasses, three eggs, three even teaspoons soda, two small teaspoons ginger. Stir butter and sugar together; then add the other ingredients, with flour enough to make a soft dough. Roll thick, cut, and bake in a quick oven.

MRS. GEORGE F. HURD.

GINGER COOKIES.

One-half cup butter, one cup brown sugar, one cup molasses, one cup sour milk, one teaspoon ginger, one-half teaspoon cinnamon, one-half teaspoon nutmeg, one egg, one quart flour, one teaspoon saleratus dissolved in the milk. Bake in cups. Very nice hot for tea.

MRS. G. DARLING.

GINGER SNAPS.

One cup of molasses, one cup of sugar. Put four table-spoons of boiling water into a cup and fill the cup with melted butter. One teaspoon of ginger, one of salt and one of soda. Mix as soft as you can roll out; roll as thin as a knife blade.

COOKIES.

One cup sugar, two-thirds cup butter, two tablespoons sour milk, one large egg or two small ones, a little soda.

RAISED DOUGHNUTS.

One pint sweet milk, one-half pint lard, one pint sugar, three eggs. Mix soft at night, using the milk, one-half the sugar and lard and one-half pint of yeast. In the morning add the rest with the eggs, one nutmeg, two tablespoons whiskey, and a little soda. Knead well, and raise; when light, roll out thin, and after cutting let raise again before frying. One-half beef suet and one-half lard is better to fry them in than all lard.   MRS. WOODBURY.

DOUGHNUTS.

One and one-half coffeecup sugar, one-half coffeecup lard, one and one-half coffeecup milk, three eggs, four teaspoons baking powder, one teaspoon salt, one nutmeg, flour enough to mix soft.

FRIED CAKES.

One cup of sugar, one cup of sweet milk, three table-spoons of butter, three teaspoons of baking powder, two eggs, one quart of flour.   MRS. W. T. MILLS.

CRULLERS.

One cup sour cream, one cup sugar, one egg, small tea-spoon soda, a little salt; spice to taste. Mix soft. Fry in boiling lard.   AUNT JANE.

COMFORTS.

One cup milk, one cup sugar, two eggs, a little salt, two and one-half cups of flour, three teaspoons baking powder. Mix thoroughly, and drop from a spoon into boiling lard; fry a light brown.   MRS. CANDEE.

PEPPERNUTS.

One pound flour, one pound sugar, four eggs, one teaspoon cloves, one of cinnamon, one-half pound citron, one cup blanched almonds, one-half teaspoon black pepper, one-half teaspoon salt. Rub flour and sugar together; add the other ingredients. Roll out and cut in small square cakes. Bake a light brown.   MRS. WINANS.

ANGEL FOOD.

One gill flour, one and one-half gills sugar, the whites of eleven eggs, one teaspoon of cream tartar (just even full), one teaspoon of vanilla. Beat the eggs to a stiff froth, then add sugar after sifting twice; sift the flour five times and mix the cream tartar in it well; put a pan in the oven and set your tin on that, or it will bake too fast. Bake in a new tin and do not grease. Time one hour in a slow oven. A very nice and delicate cake.   MRS. A. PRENTICE.

LADY FINGERS.

One-half pound pulverized sugar and six yolks of eggs, well stirred; add one-fourth pound flour, whites of six eggs, well beaten. Bake in lady finger tins, or squeeze through a bag of paper in strips two or three inches long. These are nice placed together after baking, with frosting or chocolate icing.   I. M. S.

FRUIT JUMBLES.

One cup butter, two cups sugar, three and one-half cups flour, one-half cup milk, three eggs, one-half nutmeg, grated; three teaspoons baking powder, one cup currants. Bake in a broad shallow tin, and cut in squares while warm.
        MRS. EMMA W. SAGE.

ECLAIRS A LA CREME.

Three-fourths pound flour, one pint water, ten eggs, one-half cup butter. Put the water on the fire in a stew-pan with the butter; as soon as it boils stir in the sifted flour; stir well until it leaves the bottom and sides of the pan, when taken from the fire; then add the eggs one at a time. Put the batter in a bag of paper, and press out in the shape of fingers on a greased tin. When cold fill with cream.

CREAM.

One and one-half pints milk, two cups sugar, yolks of five eggs, one tablespoon butter, three large tablespoons corn starch, two teaspoons extract vanilla. They are very nice frosted with chocolate.

I. M. S.

SCOTCH SHORT BREAD.

Four pounds flour, two and one-half pounds butter, one and one-fourth pounds sugar, one wine glass rose water, one-half pound caraway comfits, one-half pound citron. Rub the butter and sugar to a cream, add the rose water, then the flour; roll out rather less than one-half an inch in thickness, and strew the comfits and citron on the top; pass the rolling pin over them, and then cut into squares and diamonds with a paste jigger. Good for three months.

Mrs. M. K. W.

BREAD CAKE.

Two coffee cups bread dough, two teacups sugar, two eggs, one teacup butter, two teaspoons essence lemon, one nutmeg, teaspoon each cloves, cinnamon and allspice, wine glass brandy, coffee cup raisins. Let rise before baking.

Mrs. A. S. Lane.

COFFEE CAKE.

One cup brown sugar, one cup molasses, one cup butter, one cup strained coffee, wine glass brandy, one pound raisins, one pound currants, one tablespoon cinnamon, one tablespoon cloves, two nutmegs, one teaspoon soda, four cups flour.

MRS. L. WINANS.

FRUIT CAKE WITHOUT EGGS.

One pound fat pork, chopped fine; pour over it one pint boiling water or coffee, two cups molasses, one cup sugar, one and one-half pound raisins, one-half pound currants one tablespoon cinnamon, one teaspoon saleratus, eight cups flour.   · MRS. H. DOTY.

RAISED LOAF CAKE.

Four cups flour, one cup butter, one-half cup yeast, one cup milk; let it raise over night, then add two cups sugar, two eggs, one-half teaspoon saleratus, one pound raisins; put in tins; let rise again and bake.

MRS. FLINT.

NUT CAKE.

Two eggs, one cup sugar, one-half cup butter, one-half cup sweet milk, one and one-half cups sifted flour, two teaspoons baking powder, one large cup chopped walnuts. Frost when baked, mark in squares and put half a nut on each square.   MRS. MATTIE C. DAYFOOT.

NUT CAKE.

Two-thirds cup butter, two cups sugar, one cup milk. three eggs, three cups flour, three teaspoons baking powder, one cup nuts; bake in shallow tins about two inches thick, cut in squares, frost and put walnut meat on each piece.

E. B.

POUND CAKE.

One and one-half cups flour, one cup butter, one and one-half cups sugar, one cup eggs, one-half teaspoon baking powder. Beat butter and flour to a cream; beat the eggs and sugar very light; put all together and add the baking powder. Mrs. M. K. Woodbury.

WHITE CAKE.

One cup butter, two cups sugar, two and one-half cups flour, one-half cup sweet milk, whites eight eggs, two teaspoons baking powder. Mrs. W.

ALMOND CAKE.

Two cups sugar, three cups flour, one cup butter, one-half cup sour milk, whites of eight eggs, two teaspoons baking powder, one teaspoon bitter almonds, one cup blanched almonds. Mrs. A. Churchill.

SNOW CAKE.

One cup sugar, one and one-half cups flour, two teaspoons cream tartar. Sift all together through a sieve; add the whites of ten eggs beaten stiff. Bake in a quick oven. Mrs. E. W. Sage.

LEMON CUP CAKE.

One cup butter, three cups sugar, five cups flour, one cup milk, one teaspoon saleratus, six eggs, peel and juice of one lemon. Mrs. C.

IMPERIAL CAKE.

One pound sugar, one pound butter, one pound flour, two pounds raisins, one pound citron, one pound sweet almonds, two tablespoons wine or brandy, one nutmeg, mace, ten eggs. Mrs. C.

CORN STARCH CAKE.

One-half cup butter, one and one-half cups sugar, one and one-half cups flour, one-half cup corn starch, one-half cup milk, whites six eggs, one and one-half teaspoons baking powder, a few blanched and chopped almonds.

CLAY CAKE.

One pound sugar, one pound flour, one-half pound butter, six eggs, one-half pint sweet cream, one and one-half teaspoons baking powder, little nutmeg.

SODA POUND CAKE.

One and one-half coffeecups sugar, three fourths coffeecup butter, two coffeecups flour, one-half coffeecup milk, four eggs, one and one-half teaspoon baking powder. Flavor with lemon.

SPONGE CAKE.

One pint flour, one pint sugar, six eggs, one-half cup water, three teaspoons baking powder. Mix the yolks and sugar, then add the water, then flour, then the whites of eggs on top. Stir as little as possible.

L. B.

SPONGE CAKE.

One pound of sugar, one-half pound flour, a little salt, ten eggs ; flavor with lemon or vanilla.

MRS. W. N. S.

FEATHER SPONGE CAKE.

One and one-half goblets sifted sugar, one goblet sifted flour, two teaspoons cream tartar, one-half teaspoon salt. Sift all through a sieve ; add whites of ten eggs well beaten. Bake in two square tins in quick oven, frost, flavoring with bitter almond or rose.   JENNIE.

SPONGE CAKE.

One cup of sugar, one cup flour, mix thoroughly; four eggs (beaten separately), mix the whites in first; two teaspoons baking powder, little salt, lemon or vanilla.

Mrs. W. T. Mills.

QUEEN'S CAKE.

One pound sugar, one pound flour, one-half pound butter, four eggs, one and one half gills sour cream, one gill wine or brandy, one nutmeg, small teaspoon soda, one pound raisins, one-half pound citron.

WASHINGTON CAKE.

Three cups sugar, two cups butter, one cup milk or water, four cups flour, five eggs, three teaspoons baking powder, one pound raisins, one-half pound citron, one teaspoon ground cinnamon, one nutmeg.

Mrs. Ambrose Lane.

SPICE CAKE.

One cup butter, two cups brown sugar, three and one-half cups flour, one cup cold water, two teaspoons baking powder, three eggs, two teaspoons cinnamon, one-half teaspoon cloves, one-half nutmeg, one large cup raisins and currants.

Mrs. H. E. Birdseye.

JUMBLE CAKE.

One cup butter, two cups sugar, one cup sour milk, and one-half teaspoon soda, one nutmeg, five eggs, little less than one quart flour, two teaspoons baking powder.

COCOANUT CAKE.

Three-fourths pound butter, one pound sugar, three-fourths pound flour, eight eggs, the grated meat of a cocoanut.

C. U.

COCOANUT CAKE.

One pound sugar, one-half pound flour, two teaspoons baking powder, one-half pound butter, six eggs or whites of twelve, two grated cocoanuts, save enough of it for the frosting, put the rest in the cake.   Will make one large cake.

MRS. FANNIE B. NORTHROP.

WHITE CAKE.

One-half cup butter, two cups sugar, one cup milk, three cups flour, whites four eggs, two teaspoons baking powder.

MRS. A. A. MORGAN.

COMPOSITION CAKE.

One pound of flour, three-fourths pound of sugar, one-half pound of butter, three eggs, one-half pint of sweet milk, one-half teaspoon of soda, one nutmeg, a little cloves, one glass of brandy, one pound of fruit.   If you wish the cake rich, add as much more fruit as you like.

LEMON CAKE.

One and one-half cups of sugar, one-half cup of butter, one-half cup of milk, two cups of flour, two eggs, juice and grated rind of one lemon, one-half teaspoon of soda.

WHITE FRUIT CAKE.

Whites of eight eggs, two cups sugar, one cup butter, one cup milk, four cups flour, two teaspoons baking powder, two cups raisins, one-half cup citron, sliced fine.

MRS. EMMA W. SAGE.

WEDDING CAKE.

One pound flour, one pound butter, one and one-half pounds brown sugar, twelve eggs, eleven pounds raisins, two pounds citron, one-half ounce cinnamon, three-fourths ounce cloves, one ounce mace, three gills brandy, one teacup milk, two teaspoons baking powder.

WEDDING FRUIT CAKE.

One pound flour, one pound sugar, one pound butter, two pounds currants, one pound raisins, one-half pound citron, one ounce mace, one ounce cinnamon, four nutmegs, one ounce cloves, eight eggs, wineglass brandy, one-half ounce rose water.   MRS. ALFRED S. LANE.

WEDDING FRUIT CAKE.

One pound butter, one pound brown sugar, one pound flour, slightly browned; twelve eggs, six pounds raisins, four pounds currants, one pound citron, four nutmegs, one tablespoon mace, two tablespoons cinnamon, one-half tablespoon cloves, two wineglasses white wine, two wineglasses brandy, one wineglass rose water.

MRS. H. E. B.

WHITE FROSTING.

To the white of an egg when thoroughly beaten, add five tablespoons sugar, beating all the time. Will frost one medium sized cake.

CHOCOLATE FROSTING.

Whites of three eggs, fifteen tablespoons pulverized sugar, four tablespoons grated chocolate. Beat whites thoroughly; add the sugar and chocolate.

COCOANUT FROSTING.

Whites of three eggs, twelve tablespoons sugar, one grated cocoanut. Beat the sugar and eggs together ; spread on the cake, and sprinkle the cocoanut over thickly. This will make a whiter frosting than stirring in the cocoanut.

ORANGE ICING.

Whites of two eggs, twelve tablespoons sugar, two oranges, grated.

LEMON ICING.

Whites of two eggs, two cups sugar, juice and part of the rind of two lemons.

ALMOND ICING.

The whites of three eggs, beaten light ; one cup of blanched almonds, chopped fine or pounded ; ten tablespoons pulverized sugar. Flavor with little bitter almond.

COOKED FROSTING.

One small teacup of granulated sugar, wet with very little water. Set on the stove and let it boil, without stirring, until it begins to thicken. Take whites of two eggs, beat very light. Strain the boiled sugar into them slowly, beating all the time. Flavor to taste.

MARTHA WASHINGTON CAKE.

One cup sugar, one cup sweet milk, two cups flour, one egg, two teaspoons baking powder, two tablespoons butter. Bake in three layers.

CUSTARD.

One egg, one-half pint milk, one teaspoon corn starch, one tablespoon flour, two tablespoons sugar. Scald the milk ; beat the sugar, flour, egg and corn starch together ; add the milk, boil until thick. Flavor, and when cold, spread between cake.   MRS. CANDEE.

ALMOND CREAM CAKE.

Two cups sugar (pulverized), one-fourth cup butter, one cup sweet milk, three cups flour, three teaspoons baking powder, whites four eggs, beaten very light; one-half teaspoon vanilla. Bake in four layers.

FOR THE CREAM.

Whip one cup of sweet cream to a froth; stir gradually into it one-half cup pulverized sugar, a few drops vanilla, and one pound of almonds, blanched and chopped. Spread quite thickly between the layers of cake, and frost the top and sides.

MRS. HENRY BARNARD.

JELLY FRUIT CAKE.

Two cups sugar, three cups flour, three teaspoons baking powder, two-thirds cup butter, one cup milk, three eggs. Flavor with vanilla. To half the cake add one tablespoon molasses, one tablespoon brandy, one tablespoon cinnamon, one teaspoon cloves, one-half teaspoon allspice, one-half nutmeg, one cup chopped raisins, one-half pound citron. Bake in jelly tins, two layers of light and two of fruit cake. Spread jelly between the layers, when slightly cool, putting a light one on top. Over all spread white frosting.

H. A.

CONFECTIONERY CAKE.

One coffeecup sugar, three-fourths coffeecup butter, two coffeecups flour, one coffeecup milk, whites five eggs, three teaspoons baking powder. Flavor with vanilla. Take one tablespoon of this cake, add one-half cup chopped raisins, one-half cup citron, one-half cup flour, one-half cup molasses, two teaspoons cinnamon, one-half teaspoon cloves, one wineglass brandy. Bake in three layers, two light and one dark. Put together with soft frosting.

MRS WM. HURD.

BLACK CHOCOLATE CAKE.

One cup butter, two cups sugar, two and one-half cups flour, five eggs, one cup sour milk, one teaspoon soda dissolved in a little boiling water; one-half cake "Baker's" chocolate, grated and put in the cake before stirring in the flour. Bake in jelly tins in four layers.

FILLING.

One pound white sugar wet with a little cold water; add the whites of three eggs, slightly beaten; one-half cake grated chocolate. Cook in boiling water until it thickens. Flavor with vanilla. Spread between the layers, and outside the cake. Sprinkle grated cocoanut over the top.

MRS. J. A. S.

LEMON COCOANUT CAKE.

One pound sugar, one pound flour, one-half pound butter, six eggs, one-half pint cream, one teaspoon cream tartar, one-half teaspoon soda.

DRESSING BETWEEN LAYERS.

One grated cocoanut, three-fourths cup sugar, two eggs, juice of one lemon. Beat the eggs thoroughly, add sugar and lemon, lastly the cocoanut; put all on the stove and cook enough to cook the egg, being careful not to burn. Frost the cake and strew cocoanut over the top.

MRS. GILBERT.

JELLY CAKE.

One-half cup butter, two cups sugar, one cup sweet milk, three and one-half cups flour, and three teaspoons baking powder, four eggs. Flavor with lemon or vanilla. Bake in jelly tins.

MRS. W. T. MILLS

GERMAN CAKE.

One cup sugar, two tablespoons butter, one cup flour, four eggs, one teaspoon baking powder. Bake in two layers.

FILLING.

Whites of five eggs, fifteen tablespoons sugar; add grated cocoanut. Spread between and on top of layers.

MRS. A. S. MANN.

ORANGE CAKE.

Two cups sugar, one cup butter, one cup sweet milk, three cups flour, five eggs (yolks of two and whites of five); three teaspoons baking powder, two oranges (grated peel and juice of one). Bake in four layers.

FILLING.

Whites of three eggs, juice of one orange, fifteen table-spoons of sugar. Beat together, spread between layers and outside of cake. Pare and pull in small pieces two oranges; put on top of cake.

BELLE.

WHITE MOUNTAIN CAKE.

One cup sugar, one-half cup of butter, one half cup sweet milk, one-half cup corn starch, one cup flour, whites of six eggs, a little vanilla, two teaspoons baking powder. Bake in layers.

FROSTING FOR ABOVE.

Whites of five eggs, twenty tablespoons sifted sugar, beaten very light; a little vanilla. Spread between layers and outside of cake.

PICKLES, CANNED FRUIT, Etc.

CUCUMBER PICKLES.

Make a weak brine, hot or cold; if hot, let the cucumbers stand in it twenty-four hours, if cold forty-eight hours; rinse, and dry the cucumbers with a cloth, take vinegar enough to cover them, allow one ounce of alum to every gallon of vinegar, put it in a brass kettle with the cucumbers and heat slowly, turning the cucumbers from the bottom frequently; as soon as they are heated through skim them out into a crock, let the vinegar boil up, turn it over the pickles and let them stand at least twenty-four hours; drain off the vinegar. Take fresh vinegar, and to every gallon allow two table-spoons of white mustard seed, one of cloves, one of celery seed, one of stick cinnamon, one large green pepper, a very little horse radish, and if you like one-half pint sugar. Divide the spices equally into several small bags of coarse muslin, scald with the vinegar and pour over the pickles. If you like your pickles hard, let the vinegar cool before pouring over them.

PICKLED CUCUMBERS.
FOR ONE THOUSAND.

Sprinkle salt and pour boiling water over for three successive days, then prepare vinegar as follows: One-fourth pound whole cloves, one-fourth pound cinnamon, one-fourth pound allspice, one fourth pound black pepper, one-fourth pound white mustard, alum size of an egg, one pound brown sugar, a little horse radish root. Boil with vinegar ten minutes and pour over pickles; put the spices in a bag or leave loose in vinegar, as you choose.   M. C.

CUCUMBER PICKLES.

SIX HUNDRED CUCUMBERS.

Make a brine that will bear up an egg, beat it boiling hot, pour it over the cucumbers; let them stand twenty-four hours, or make a cold brine and let it stand forty-eight hours. Take the cucumbers and wipe the black specks from each one, then take sufficient quantity of vinegar to cover them, and add a small lump of alum; put the cucumbers in the brass kettle with the vinegar cold, heat them slowly, turning them from the bottom several times; let them stand twenty-four hours; afterwards take three gallons of vinegar if needed to cover them; the size of the cucumbers vary so much, judgment must be used. Then put three pints of brown sugar, three gills of mustard seed, a handful of cloves, a handful of stick cinnamon, six green peppers, one tablespoon of celery seed, ginger root, a piece of alum the size of a walnut; tie in a muslin bag all the spices, with the peppers, and scald with the vinegar, then pour it over the cucumbers hot; add green grapes and horse radish, cold.

MRS. OREN SAGE.

EAST INDIA PICKLE.

One hundred cucumbers (large and small), one peck green tomatoes, one-half peck onions, four cauliflowers, four red peppers (without the seeds), four heads celery, one pint bottle horseradish. Slice all, and stand in salt twenty-four hours; then drain, pour on weak vinegar, stand on stove until it comes to a boil; then drain again. One ounce ground cinnamon, one ounce ground turmeric, one-half pound mustard, one-quarter pound brown sugar; wet these with cold vinegar; add to this sufficient vinegar to moisten all the pickles. Cook all together ten minutes. Seal in bottles while hot.

MRS. PITKIN.

FRENCH PICKLE.

One peck green tomatoes, sliced; six large onions, a tea-cup of salt thrown on over night. Drain thoroughly, then boil in two quarts of water and one quart of vinegar fifteen or twenty minutes; drain in colander; then take four quarts vinegar, two pounds brown sugar, one-half pound white mustard seed, two tablespoons cloves, two tablespoons cinnamon, two tablespoons ginger, two tablespoons ground mustard, one teaspoon cayenne pepper; put all together and cook fifteen minutes.   M. C.

PICCALLILY.

One peck green tomatoes sliced, one-half peck onions sliced, one cauliflower, one peck small cucumbers. Leave in salt and water twenty-four hours; then put in kettle with handful scraped horseradish, one ounce turmeric, one ounce cloves (whole), one-quarter pound pepper (whole), one ounce cassia buds or cinnamon, one pound white mustard seed, one pound English mustard. Put in kettle in layers, and cover with cold vinegar. Boil fifteen minutes, constantly stirring.

HIGDOM.

One-half dozen large cucumbers, one dozen small cucumbers, one-half dozen large onions, two dozen green tomatoes, one cabbage, four large green peppers, two large red peppers; chop fine, and sprinkle over a coffee cup of salt; let it stand over night, then drain through a colander. Put two quarts of vinegar, one quart of water with this, and boil fifteen minutes; drain again, and add one pound brown sugar, one-half pound white mustard seed, three tablespoons cloves, three tablespoons cinnamon, two tablespoons allspice, two tablespoons ginger, two tablespoons mustard, one small teaspoon cayenne pepper, one small teaspoon black pepper, alum size of a walnut; add vinegar enough to cover all. Let it just boil.   M. C.

TOMATO SOY.

One-half bushel green tomatoes, three onions, three green peppers, one-quarter pound mustard seed, three cups sugar, three cabbages. Chop the tomatoes and onions together (fine) ; add to one gallon of the tomatoes one cup of salt ; let stand twenty-four hours, drain and add the peppers (chopped fine), mustard seed, sugar and other spices, to taste. Moisten all with vinegar and cook until tender. Before bottling, add the cabbages (chopped), and one cup chopped horseradish.

CHILI SAUCE.

One peck ripe tomatoes, six green peppers, six onions, two teaspoons ground allspice, two teaspoons ground cloves, two teaspoons ground cinnamon, two cups brown sugar, five cups vinegar, salt to taste. Scald and skim the tomatoes, chop the onions and peppers fine ; boil all together slowly, three or four hours, then bottle.

MRS. LANE.

CHOW CHOW.

One quart large cucumbers, one quart small cucumbers, two quarts onions, four heads cauliflower, six green peppers, one quart green tomatoes, one gallon vinegar, one pound mustard, two cups sugar, two cups flour, one ounce turmeric. Put all in salt and water one night ; cook all the vegetables in brine until tender, except large cucumbers. Pour vinegar and spices over.

TOMATO CATSUP.

One gallon of tomatoes (strained), six tablespoons salt, three tablespoons black pepper, one tablespoon cloves, two tablespoons cinnamon, two tablespoons allspice, one and one-half pints vinegar ; boil down one-half. One peck of tomatoes will make one gallon strained.

GREEN TOMATO CATSUP.

One peck of green tomatoes, one dozen large onions, one-half pint salt ; slice the tomatoes and onions. To a layer of these add a layer of salt ; let stand twenty-four hours, then drain. Add one-quarter pound mustard seed, three dessert-spoons sweet oil, one ounce allspice, one ounce cloves, one ounce ground mustard, one ounce ground ginger, two table-spoons black pepper, two teaspoons celery seed, one-quarter pound brown sugar. Put all ingredients in preserving pan, cover with vinegar, and boil two hours.

L. B.

TOMATO CATSUP.

One peck ripe tomatoes, cut up, boil tender and sift through a wire sieve ; add one large tablespoon ground cloves, one large tablespoon allspice, one large tablespoon cinnamon, one teaspoon cayenne pepper, one-quarter pound salt, one-quarter pound mustard, one pint vinegar. Boil gently three hours. Bottle and seal while warm.

MRS. LANE.

GRAPE CATSUP.

Five pints of grapes, simmer until soft, then put through a colander ; add to them two pints brown sugar, one pint vinegar, two tablespoons allspice, two tablespoons cinnamon, two tablespoons cloves, one and one-half teaspoons mace, one teaspoon salt, one and one-half teaspoons red pepper. Boil till thick ; then bottle.   E. & I.

RIPE CUCUMBER PICKLE.

Pare and scrape out the inside of the cucumber ; put in a weak brine for twenty-four hours. Make a syrup of sugar and vinegar ; boil a few slices of the cucumber at a time in this, until they look clear. When the cucumbers are all cooked, boil down the syrup and pour over them.

M. C.

RIPE CUCUMBER PICKLE.

Peel and take out the inside of the cucumbers; cut in pieces, put in cold vinegar, let them lie twenty-four hours; then to a quart of vinegar put two pounds of sugar and one ounce cinnamon buds. Boil the whole together, until the cucumbers are clear.

PICKLED WATERMELON.

Take the green part of the rind of the lemon, pare and cut in small pieces. To one quart of vinegar add two pounds of sugar, one ounce of cassia buds. In this boil the rind until clear and tender.

L. H.

SPICED PEACHES.

Seven pounds fruit, one pint vinegar, three pounds sugar, two ounces cinnamon, one-half ounce cloves. Scald together sugar, vinegar and spices; pour over the fruit. Let it stand twenty-four hours; drain off, scald again and pour over fruit, letting it stand another twenty-four hours. Boil all together until the fruit is tender. Skim it out and boil the liquor until thickened. Pour over the fruit and set away in a jar.

SPICED GRAPES.

Seven pounds grapes, three pounds sugar, one pint vinegar, one tablespoon cloves, one tablespoon cinnamon.

SWEET PICKLED PEACHES.

One peck peaches, three pounds brown sugar, one quart vinegar. Dip each peach in a weak solution of soda water, and wipe dry to remove roughness. Stick three or four cloves in each peach. Heat the vinegar and sugar, then put in the peaches and cook until tender.

MRS. E. S. CONVERSE.

PIKLED PEACHES.

One peck peaches, three pounds sugar, one quart vinegar, cloves.

PICKLED PLUMS.

Four pounds plums, two pounds sugar, one pint vinegar.

PICKLED PEARS.

One-half bushel pears, three quarts vinegar, five pounds sugar, cinnamon to taste.

SPICED BLACKBERRIES.

To six pints fruit take two and one-half pints sugar, one and one-half pints vinegar, one-half ounce cinnamon (ground), one-half ounce cloves, one-half ounce allspice, a little mace broken in small pieces. Boil the sugar and vinegar together, with the spices, putting these last into muslin bags. Then put in the berries and let them scald, not boil.

MRS. M. K. WOODBURY.

In canning fruit, to a pound of fruit allow one-fourth to one-half pound sugar, according to taste.

CANNED PINE APPLE.

Pare the fruit, and be very particular to cut out the eyes. Weigh it and chop fine. Add to it the same weight of sugar. Mix thoroughly in a large crock, and let it stand twenty-four hours. Then put in cans, filling them full, and seal tight. After leaving them about two weeks it is well to look and see if there are any signs of working. If so pour into a pan and warm through, then replace in tin cans.

MRS. A. S. LANE.

CANNED CHERRIES.

One-fourth pound sugar, one pound fruit, one teacup vinegar to five pounds fruit.

CANNED PINE-APPLE.

Three-fourths pound sugar to one pound of fruit. Pick the pine-apple to pieces with silver fork. Scald, and can hot.

MRS. A. S. MANN.

CURRANT JELLY.

Put the fruit on and scald thoroughly ; strain, and for one pint juice allow one pound sugar ; when juice boils, stir in sugar ; boil until dissolved. Pour into glasses.

RASPBERRY JAM.

Six pounds sugar to eight pounds fruit, one pint currant juice, with an additional pound of sugar. Jam all together, and boil down until a good, rich flavor. Then can.

MRS. A. S. MANN.

ORANGE MARMALADE.

Peel the oranges, and put peel in water; let boil until tender ; then with a knife scrape off the white lining, which is bitter ; then cut up peel fine. Take the oranges, divide into sections as they separate naturally. With a pair of scissors cut off the stringy edge in middle of piece, the seeds will then come out easily. Chop or cut fine, and add to peel. Then to one pint of orange, add one pound of sugar, and boil until thick enough ; it thickens a little in cooling.

J. M.

SALADS.

CABBAGE SALAD.

To a dish of chopped cabbage, four teaspoons of celery seed, or one bunch of celery. Put in a bowl, yolks of two eggs, one teaspoon of sugar, one teaspoon of butter, one teaspoon of pepper, one teaspoon of salt, one teaspoon of made mustard, one-half teacup of vinegar. Set the bowl into hot water, stir carefully until it begins to thicken. Let it get cold. Pour over the cabbage. If it does not moisten it enough, put in a little more vinegar.   MRS. W. T. M.

CABBAGE SALAD.

Two cabbages, chopped fine; sprinkle with salt; let stand over night. One pint vinegar, one-half cup ground mustard, three eggs. Beat eggs thoroughly and add to boiling vinegar. Wet the mustard with cold water or vinegar; add to the boiling vinegar; pepper and salt to taste, and let all come to a boil. Pour over cabbage, and stir thoroughly together.

MRS. M. B. BIRDSEYE.

DRESSING FOR CABBAGE.

One egg, one teaspoon mustard, one teaspoon salt, one teaspoon sugar, one-half cup vinegar, one-half cup milk.

SALAD DRESSING.

Beat four eggs light, add one tablespoon mixed mustard, one-half teaspoon salt, five tablespoons vinegar, a little cayenne pepper; mix well, then stand in a dish filled with boiling water; when warmed through add a tablespoon of butter; cook until a little thicker than custard, stirring constantly. If desired it may be boiled until thicker, then thinned with milk or cream.   MRS. GILBERT.

SALAD DRESSING.

Yolk of one egg, salt-spoon of salt, mustard-spoon of mustard, one cruet of oil put in very slowly, and when well beaten add one tablespoon of vinegar.

CHICKEN SALAD.

Boil the white meat of two large chickens; cut it coarse, and add the white part of celery cut coarse; a little more chicken than celery.

DRESSING.

Three yolks of eggs, well beaten; one pint of oil added drop by drop, and beaten; the juice of two lemons, one teaspoon of dry mustard, a little cayenne pepper, a little salt. If not moist enough beat the whites of two eggs and add to it.

MRS. GEO. GOULD.

CHICKEN SALAD.

Use the white meat of two good sized chickens, and celery enough to make the proportion one-third chicken and two-thirds celery; boil ten eggs hard, rub the yolks perfectly smooth with a silver spoon, adding gradually four tablespoons of olive oil, one tablespoon of made mustard, two teaspoons of salt, one teaspoon of black pepper, half a teaspoon of cayenne pepper, and one tablespoon of sugar; add sweet cream by degrees until about the consistency of batter. Just before sending to table, mix the dressing with the chicken and celery, and moisten with sharp vinegar. The juice of two lemons is an improvement.

MRS. W. N. SAGE.

MAYONAISE DRESSING.

Yolks of three eggs, beaten, oil added gradually until as stiff as cake-batter; salt-spoon of salt, lastly the white of one egg, beaten stiff. This is very nice for lobster or chicken salad, or as a dressing for celery. MRS. G. D.

SALMON SALAD.

One can fresh salmon, four bunches celery; chop as for chicken salad; mix with the salmon.

DRESSING.

One teaspoon of mustard, two tablespoons vinegar, yolks of two eggs, salt to taste, and a little cayenne pepper; mix thoroughly, add it to the salmon just before serving.

Mrs. C. F. PAINE.

BEVERAGES.

VIENNA COFFEE.

Equal parts Mocha and Java coffee; allow one heaping tablespoon of coffee to each person, and two extra to make good strength; mix one egg with the grounds, pour on the coffee half as much boiling water as will be needed, let the coffee froth, then stir down the grounds, and let it boil five minutes; then let the coffee stand where it will keep hot, but not boil, for five or ten minutes, and add the rest of the water. To one pint of cream add the white of an egg, well beaten; this is to be put in the cups with the sugar, and the hot coffee added.

Mrs. A. W. MUDGE.

KAOKA COFFEE.

Put into an ordinary tea or coffee pot the same quantity of K. O. K. as would be used of coffee, pour on sufficient boiling water to extract the strength, letting boil fifteen minutes, after which add enough boiling water for the requirements of the family, remove from the stove and let settle for a few moments; milk or cream and sugar to taste. It will be found to improve by long simmering on the stove, but be sure to let it settle before using. Do not throw away any of the clear liquid, but heat it up again and add to the next brewing; it is even better than the first.

ELLEN'S COFFEE.
FOR SIX PERSONS.

Take one full cup ground coffee, one egg, a little cold water; stir together, add one pint boiling water, boil up; then add another pint boiling water, and set back to settle before serving.

TEA.

One teaspoon of tea is allowed for each person; pour on a little boiling water and let come to a boil; add as much hot water as is necessary.

CHOCOLATE.

Tablespoon chocolate for each person. Pour on boiling water and allow to thicken up; milk enough to cool; then stir in well beaten egg and sugar to taste, add milk and boil fifteen or twenty minutes; flavor with vanilla. Beat whites of eggs and pour over them when ready to serve.

WINE WHEY.

One pint sweet milk, boil, and pour sherry wine until it curdles; then strain and use the whey.   E. H. H.

BLACK CURRANT CORDIAL.

Five quarts black currants, two ounces ginger root, one ounce cloves, two ounces stick cinnamon, two ounces allspice, four nutmegs, one teaspoon cayenne pepper. Bruise the currants, the ginger root and cinnamon, add all the other spices except pepper. Put into a thin muslin bag; put the pepper in another bag; pour over all one-half gallon whiskey. Let it stand forty-eight hours, stirring occasionally; strain this off, and put over the currants another half gallon of whiskey; stir thoroughly, and strain into the other whiskey; add to this liquor four pounds granulated sugar. If too strong, dilute with a little water; then bottle.

GRANDMA REID.

BOULLION.

Two pounds lean beef, chopped fine; pour over it one quart cold water, put in a porcelain kettle, cover tight, and let it simmer four hours. Strain off the tea and let it cool, beat the white of one egg and add to the tea; put in on the stove and stir until it comes to a boil; let it boil until it becomes perfectly clear, skimming; then strain through a fine napkin; season with salt to taste.

MRS. EDGAR HOLMES.

RASPBERRY VINEGAR.

Cut the berries with vinegar; let them stand forty-eight hours. Strain them through a sieve; add one pound white sugar to one pint of juice; boil one-half hour, then bottle. If possible, use half red berries; they give a richer flavor, and the black ones the color.

MRS. A. LANE.

RASPBERRY VINEGAR.

Three pints red berries; pour over them one pint cider vinegar and let stand twenty-four hours. Strain, and to one pint of juice add one pound of sugar; boil one-half hour, and when cold, bottle for use.

MRS. HIRAM DOTY.

SWEETS.

GENERAL DIRECTIONS.

Granulated sugar is preferable. Candy should not be stirred while boiling. Cream tartar should not be added until the syrup begins to boil. Butter should be put in when the candy is almost done. Flavors are more delicate when not boiled in the candy.

CREAM FOR BON-BONS.

Three cups sugar, one and one-half cups water, one-half teaspoon cream tartar; flavor with vanilla. Boil until drops will almost keep their shape in water; then pour into a bowl set in cold water; stir steadily with a silver or wooden spoon until cool enough to bear the hand; then place on a platter and knead until of fine even texture. If too hard, a few drops of warm water may be stirred in; if too soft, it must be boiled again. This is the general foundation of Cream Bon-Bons. It must be flavored with chocolate, by adding a tablespoon of melted chocolate while the syrup is hot.

MISS HELEN W. HOOKER.

CHOCOLATE CREAMS.

Set one-half cake cooking chocolate on a plate or flat dish, in the oven until soft. Prepare the cream (as cream bon-bons); roll into small balls; leave a few moments to dry, then roll in the melted chocolate and place on buttered paper. Two two-tined forks will be found most convenient for rolling in the chocolate. H. W. H.

CHOCOLATE CREAMS.

One-half cup water, one-half cake chocolate, two cups sugar; flavor with lemon or vanilla. Boil the sugar and water to a thick syrup, put aside until a little cool, then beat to a thick cream; add flavoring and make it into balls. Dip quickly into melted chocolate, place on buttered plate, and put in a cool place to dry.

MISS NELLIE SIDDONS.

ALMOND CREAMS.

Boil sugar, water, etc., as directed for cream, and when partially stirred, add a cup of blanched almonds (chopped fine). Treat as plain cream, and when well moulded, cut in squares or bars. Almond cream is very nice flavored with chocolate. H. W. H.

COCOANUT CREAM.

Make like almond cream, substituting grated or desiccated cocoanut for the almonds.   H. W. H.

CREAM ALMONDS.

Take enough of the plain cream in the hand to cover an almond, and roll the almond up in it. Almonds thus prepared, look and keep better, if rolled in powdered sugar. They are very nice made with chocolate flavored cream.

H. W. H.

COCOANUT DROPS.

One pound cocoanut (grated and dried), one pound white sugar, two eggs (well beaten). Mix this together, make them up pear shape; lay on a sheet of paper on a tin, about an inch apart. Bake fifteen minutes.

COCOANUT CREAM CANDY.

One cocoanut, one and one-half pounds granulated sugar. Put the sugar and the milk of the cocoanut together and heat slowly until the sugar is melted; then boil for five minutes; add the cocoanut (finely grated), and boil for ten minutes longer, stirring constantly to keep from burning. Pour on buttered plates, and cut in squares. Will take about two days to harden.   NELLIE SIDDONS.

CREAM WALNUTS.

Two cups sugar, two-thirds cup water. Boil without stirring, until it will spin a thread; flavor with vanilla. Set off into a dish with a little cold water in; stir briskly until white and creamy. Have the walnuts shelled; make the cream into small round cakes with your fingers; press half a walnut on either side, and drop into sifted granulated sugar. For cream dates, take fresh California dates, remove the stones and fill the centre of dates with this same cream. Drop into sugar.

A. H.

HICKORY NUT CANDY.

One cup hickory nut meats, two cups sugar, one-half cup water. Boil sugar and water without stirring, until thick enough to spin a thread. Flavor; set off into cold water; stir quickly until white, then stir in the hickory nuts; turn into a flat tin, and when cold cut into small squares.

FRUIT CANDY.

One cocoanut, one and one-half pounds granulated sugar (wet with milk of cocoanut). Put in sauce pan, let it heat slowly; then boil rapidly five minutes; add the cocoanut (grated very fine), and boil ten minutes, stirring constantly. Try a little on a cold plate, and if it forms a firm paste when cool, take from the fire. Pour part of it out on to a large tin lined with greased paper; then add to the remaining cream one-quarter pound raisins (stoned), one-half pound blanched almonds, one pint pecans, one-half cup chopped walnuts. Pour over the other cream, and when cool cut in bars and squares.   MRS. NELSON SAGE.

VANILLA CREAM CANDY.

Three cups sugar, one and one-half cups water, one-half teaspoon cream tartar, butter size of a walnut; flavor with vanilla. Boil until it begins to thread, or until the drops are somewhat brittle if dropped in cold water; pour into buttered platters, and when sufficiently cool pull over a hook, or in the hands. It may be flavored with peppermint, lemon, &c. If chocolate flavoring is desired, grate it over the hot candy, or place some melted chocolate on it before pulling. A pretty variety may be made by pulling the vanilla and chocolate candies together a few times, thus leaving it striped. Pulled candy should never be moved, after pouring into platters, until ready for pulling. It will be sure to granulate.
                                    H. W. H.

CREAM CANDY.

One pound white sugar, three tablespoons vinegar, one teaspoon lemon extract, one teaspoon cream tartar. Add a little water to moisten the sugar, and boil until brittle. Put in the extract; then turn quickly out on buttered plates. When cool, pull until white, and cut in squares.

Miss N. SIDDONS.

BUTTER SCOTCH.

Two cups sugar, two tablespoons water, piece of butter the size of an egg. Boil without stirring, until it hardens on a spoon. Pour out on buttered plates to cool.

HATTIE.

CHOCOLATE CARAMELS.

Three cups brown sugar, one cup milk, one-half cake chocolate, one piece butter (size of an egg). Boil until thick; pour in a buttered pan, and when cool cut in squares.

NELLIE SIDDONS.

CHOCOLATE CARAMELS.

Two cups molasses, one cup brown sugar, one cup cream or milk, one-half pound Baker's chocolate, piece of butter size of an egg. Beat all together; boil until it thickens in water; turn into large, flat tins, well buttered. When nearly cold, cut into small squares.

MOLASSES CANDY.

Three cups yellow coffee sugar, one-half cup molasses, one cup water, one-half teaspoon cream tartar, butter the size of a walnut. Follow the directions for vanilla cream candy.

H. W. H.

MISCELLANEOUS.

BREAD AND CAKE.

Two cups of dough, two cups of brown sugar, one cup of butter, two eggs, two-thirds cup sour milk; mix one teaspoonful soda, one teaspoonful cinnamon, one teaspoonful cloves and allspice, one cup flour, one cup raisins.

MISS ELLA WILSON.

GINGER COOKIES.

One cup sugar, two cups molasses, one cup butter, three teaspoonfuls soda in one cup boiling water, two teaspoonfuls ginger.

MISS ELLA WILSON.

SPONGE CAKE.

Two cups flour, three cups fine sugar, ten eggs. Beat to a stiff froth. Grate rind and juice of one lemon. Bake in a quick oven.

MISS MARCIA ERDLE.

WHITE WINGS CAKE.

Three cups sugar, one cup butter, one cup milk, three and one-half cups flour, whites of ten eggs; one teaspoonful cream tartar, one-half teaspoonful soda, essence of almond. Excellent for either layer or loaf cake.

MISS ELLA WILSON.

RUSSIAN CREAM.

Two-thirds box of Gelatine soaked in a cup of water one-half hour; three pints of milk, one and one-half cups of sugar, six eggs. Scald the milk, add Gelatine and yolks of eggs, stir all together and boil — when boiled take off the stove. Beat whites of eggs stiff and stir into custard. Flavor with vanilla, serve with whipped cream or custard.

ORANGE CAKE.

Two cups of sugar, two cups of flour, one-half cup of water, two teaspoonfuls baking powder, a little salt, yolks of five eggs, whites of three eggs, grated rind and juice of one orange and one lemon. Beat yolks and whites separately, and stir sugar and whites of eggs together, add yolks, then water and orange, then flour and baking powder.

FROSTING.

Whites of two eggs with grated rind and juice of one orange, stiffen with sugar.   MISS ELLA WILSON.

COPPLE PUDDING.

One pint of flour, one cup of sugar, one cup of milk, two teaspoonfuls of baking powder. Bake in layers, spread raspberry jam and soft frosting between layers and over top. Serve with wine sauce.   MISS ELLEN DOYLE.

CREAM SPONGE CAKE.

Break two eggs in a cup, fill the cup with sweet cream. One cup of white sugar, one and one-half cups of flour, one teaspoonful of baking powder, flavor to taste.

MISS ELLA WILSON.

ORNAMENTAL FROSTING.

Whites of two eggs, one-half teaspoonful tartaric acid, make stiff with powdered sugar. Make a cornucopia of paper, let frosting run through small end in any design desired.

MISS ELLA WILSON.

GRAHAM BREAD.

One pint sour milk, one pint graham flour, one cup white flour, one-half cup molasses, one teaspoonful soda. Steam one hour, and brown in oven.

MISS ELLA WILSON.

ORANGE BASKETS.

Make a basket by taking inside out of orange and fill with any kind of icing you prefer.   Makes one nice course.

BRANDY PEACHES,

Four pounds of fruit, four pounds of sugar, one pint of white brandy.   Make syrup of sugar with enough water to dissolve sugar, put fruit in and let boil five minutes.   Remove fruit and boil syrup fifteen minutes, then add brandy.   Put fruit in cans and fill with syrup.   MISS ELLA WILSON.

FRENCH PICKLE.

One peck green tomatoes, eight large onions sliced, sprinkle one cup of salt through them.   Let stand over night. Drain in the morning and boil in one quart of water, and four quarts of vinegar until tender.

After boiling strain again through cloander, then take one gallon vinegar, two pounds brown sugar, one pound white mustard seed, two tablespoons grated allspice, two of cloves, two of cinnamon, two of ginger, two of mustard, one-half of cayenne pepper.   Put all together and boil one hour.

MISS ELLA WILSON.

MAYONNAISE DRESSING.

Yolks of three eggs, one tablespoonful of mustard, one tablespoonful of sugar, one-tenth teaspoonful cayenne pepper, one teaspoonful salt, small half-cup vinegar, one pint of oil. Beat yolks and dry ingredients until light.   Add a few drops of oil at a time until thick, then add more rapidly.   Then add vinegar, when done should be very thick.   Place on ice for a few hours.   Just before serving add one cup of cream.

MISS ELLA WILSON.

A nice way to dispose of pieces of roast turkey, pork, veal, etc., is to cut fine, mix with celery, and use Mayonnaise dressing.

www.ingramcontent.com/pod-product-compliance
Lightning Source LLC
Chambersburg PA
CBHW020309090426
42735CB00009B/1283